WHITE IDENTITY POLITICS

GREG JOHNSON

Counter-Currents Publishing Ltd.
San Francisco
2020

Cover image: Athena

Cover design by Kevin I. Slaughter

Published in the United States by
COUNTER-CURRENTS PUBLISHING LTD.
P.O. Box 22638
San Francisco, CA 94122
USA
http://www.counter-currents.com/

Limited Edition Hardcover ISBN: 978-1-64264-165-3
Regular Edition Hardcover ISBN: 978-1-64264-156-1
Paperback ISBN: 978-1-64264-157-8
E-book ISBN: 978-1-64264-158-5

CONTENTS

INTRODUCTION

This volume is the sequel to my #1 best-selling book *The White Nationalist Manifesto*.[1] Before you get too excited, though, I should point out that the *Manifesto* is a #1 best-seller only among *my* books, of which this is number sixteen. (I've always wanted to test people with that well-crafted ambiguity.)

In the *Manifesto*, I state my case for White Nationalism. In *White Identity Politics*, I take a step back from White Nationalism and talk about the wider trends of national populism and white identity politics, in which White Nationalism is situated.

I originally conceived this project just after I published the *Manifesto* in September of 2018. Once the book was out, I started reading a stack of new books on nationalism, populism, and white identity politics: Roger Eatwell and Matthew Goodwin's *National Populism: The Revolt Against Liberal Democracy*, Francis Fukuyama's *Identity*, and Yoram Hazony's *The Virtue of Nationalism*.[2] I soon added other books to the list, including Eric Kaufmann's *Whiteshift*, Ashley Jardina's *White Identity Politics*, and José Pedro Zúquete's *The Identitarians*.[3]

---

[1] Greg Johnson, *The White Nationalist Manifesto* (San Francisco: Counter-Currents, 2018).

[2] Roger Eatwell and Matthew Goodwin, *National Populism: The Revolt Against Liberal Democracy* (New York: Pelican, 2018); Francis Fukuyama, *Identity: Contemporary Identity Politics and the Struggle for Recognition* (London: Profile Books, 2018); Yoram Hazony, *The Virtue of Nationalism* (New York: Basic Books, 2018).

[3] Eric Kaufmann, *Whiteshift: Populism, Immigration, & the Future of White Majorities* (London: Allen Lane, 2018); Ashley Jardina, *White Identity Politics* (Cambridge: Cambridge University Press, 2019); José Pedro Zúquete, *The Identitarians: The*

I found these books quite helpful and encouraging, for they indicated a shift in the establishment's strategy in dealing with white identity politics.

Plan A was simply to task middlebrow journalists to bury us in snark. But due to the internet, especially social media, our ideas broke out and began to shape the mainstream. When Brexit passed in June of 2016 and Donald Trump was elected President of the United States in November of that year, it became clear that our ideas needed to be taken more seriously.

Plan B was to dispatch highbrow academics and "public intellectuals" to analyze our ideas and the social trends that made them resonate with greater numbers of people. None of these books managed to refute the case for white identity politics, but they revealed the intellectual weakness of the establishment and offered useful studies of some surprisingly deep-seated and powerful social trends that will make our message increasingly relevant in the coming decades.

I also discerned a Plan C in Yoram Hazony's National Conservatism Conferences in 2019 and 2020: to coopt national populism and channel its energies into establishment conservatism. This is what befell the Trump administration and the MAGA movement. Brexit, however, was finally delivered by Boris Johnson. Indeed, Johnson's election should be seen as the second Brexit referendum that the Left was clamoring for. It must really feel bad for the globalists to control the media, academia, and the mainstream political parties and still lose twice.

I ended up writing so much about these books that I had to rethink the whole project. I was faced with a choice. I could continue writing densely-argued review essays and produce a hefty volume in the range of 250 to

---

Movement against Globalism and Islam in Europe (South Bend: University of Notre Dame Press, 2018).

300 pages, or I could stick to my original plan and write a much shorter and more accessible sequel to the *Manifesto*.

I chose the latter course, so I put the review essays aside for a companion volume and decided, instead, to collect together seven lectures written from 2018 to 2020 that cover many of these topics in a more colloquial style, which is appropriate for a book that aims at a wider audience. There is some overlap between these lectures, particularly the fifth and sixth, but it could not be neatly excised, and the points are important enough to bear repeating.

Typically, my lectures are composed in three steps. First, I simply write down what I want to say. Second, when it comes time to actually say it, I generally set aside the written text and speak largely from memory. Inevitably, I forget some things but also improvise new ideas and examples on the spot. Such lectures are much fresher and more engaging than simply reading a prepared document, although they also tend to be wordier. But oddly enough, sometimes chatty texts breeze by more quickly than shorter, denser ones. Third, I have the recording of the lecture transcribed, then I prune excess verbiage and add back in the things I forgot to say, as well as new things that occur to me as I edit.

Three of these lectures only went through the first stage of this process, because I was prevented from delivering them, thus they tend to be a bit denser and drier than the rest.

The first lecture, "White Identity Politics: Inevitable, Necessary, Moral" was delivered at the Northwest Forum in Seattle on June 9, 2018, where we celebrated the eighth birthday of *Counter-Currents*, which went online on June 11, 2010.

The second lecture, "Three Pillars of White Identity Politics: Kinship, Culture, Love of One's Own," was written for the Scandza Forum in Zagreb, Croatia, on May 2, 2020, but the event was canceled due to the COVID-19 pandemic.

The third lecture, "The Very Idea of White Privilege," was written for the Scandza Forum in Oslo, Norway, on November 2, 2019. It was not delivered because the Norwegian Police Security Service somehow divined—without knowing the topic or even the title of my talk—that it was likely to cause violence, so they dispatched armed police to arrest me.[4] Apparently, arresting someone *before* he could speak for what *other* people might do had never happened before in Norway's long history.

The net result of this fool's errand is that I was the top news item in Norway for a whole weekend, and far more Norwegians heard about me and my message because I *wasn't* allowed to speak.

I had intended to reprint "The Very Idea of White Privilege" in *It's Okay to Be White: The Best of Greg Johnson*. But the "reprint" ended up coming out before the "original." There's a story behind that.

I wanted to release this book with some fanfare, so I scheduled publication for May of 2020, to coincide with the American Renaissance Conference. When the conference was canceled due to COVID-19, I rescheduled it to coincide with a Scandza Forum event in November 2020. But that too was canceled due to COVID's second wave. Rather than postpone publication yet again, I have decided to release it without fanfare or further ado.

The fourth lecture, "In Defense of Populism," was written for the Scandza Forum in Copenhagen, Denmark, on October 12, 2019. It was not delivered, because the confer-

---

[4] Greg Johnson, "Anarcho-Tyranny in Oslo," *Counter-Currents*, November 6, 2019 and "The Norwegian Police Security Service's Order to Detain Greg Johnson," *Counter-Currents*, November 15, 2019.

ence venue was besieged by Antifa protesters, preventing me from getting inside.

The fifth lecture, "National Populism Is Here to Stay," was delivered at the Etnofutur Conference in Tallinn, Estonia on February 25, 2019. The conference was organized by Blue Awakening (Sinine Äratus), the youth movement of the Conservative People's Party of Estonia (EKRE).

The sixth lecture, "Uppity White Folks and How to Reach Them," was presented in Stockholm on September 21, 2019 and in Gothenburg on September 22 to launch the Swedish translation of *The White Nationalist Manifesto*: *Det Nationalistika Manifestet*.[5] The events were organized by Education4Future. This version is based on the transcript of the Gothenburg presentation.

The seventh lecture, "The Identitarian Matrix," was presented at the Kryptis Youth Conference in Vilnius, Lithuania on February 15, 2019.

The final chapter, "The Uppity White Folks Manifesto," is an essay I prepared especially for this volume. It outlines a policy agenda to appeal to the vast constituency of what I call "uppity white folks" who think that white identity politics is inevitable, necessary, and moral, but who are not quite ready for full white ethnonationalism.

I hope this book inspires new identitarian initiatives throughout the white world.

Acknowledgements

I want to give special thanks to the organizers of the events for which these lectures were prepared. I can name but a few: Omar Filmersson, Ruuben Kaalep, Fróði Midjord, and Cyan Quinn.

Behind these names are teams of volunteers as well as

---

[5] Greg Johnson, *Det Nationalistika Manifestet*, trans. Omar Filmersson (Helsingborg: Logik Förlag, 2019).

the audiences, who must remain anonymous, although we could not have done anything without them.

I also want to thank the people who made this book possible, from the audio-visual teams who recorded my lectures, to the volunteers who transcribed them, to the people who helped me publish them online and in book form: Scott Weisswald, John Morgan, Alex Graham, James O'Meara, Collin Cleary, Kevin Slaughter, and many others who must remain anonymous.

The cover image is my homage to Alasdair MacIntyre's *After Virtue*, one of the most mind-expanding books I read as an undergraduate.

I am grateful to Kerry Bolton, F. Roger Devlin, Sam Dickson, Ricardo Duchesne, Margot Metroland, and Tito Perdue for their splendid promotional quotes.

I owe special thanks to the generous donors who made this book possible, including David F., S.J., Tito Perdue, David Stephensen, and Charles Synyard.

This book is dedicated to Omar Filmersson, Daniel Höglund, Stefan Jacobsson, and Fróði Midjord, both in friendship and in thanks for their important metapolitical work in Scandinavia.

October 15, 2020

WHITE IDENTITY POLITICS:
INEVITABLE, NECESSARY, MORAL*

WHAT IS WHITE IDENTITY POLITICS?

White identity politics is what happens when white people in a multiracial society start thinking of themselves as a group. Whites are distinct from other racial groups, which means that at least some of our values, interests, customs, and tastes will be *different* from those of other groups. Where group differences exist in the same geographical space, group conflicts are not far behind. Where there are group conflicts, there is politics.

Politics always involves group conflicts: nation against nation, and within nations, class against class, party against party, or race against race.

White identity politics makes no sense, of course, in an all-white society. In an all-white Ireland or Iceland or Denmark, political differences might be based on class or party but not race. Many white nations had no significant non-white populations until after the Second World War, but now all white societies have some non-white populations with equal political rights. This creates the possibility of racial identity politics.

As a shorthand, I am going to use the word "identitarianism" to refer to identity politics. Just as libertarians put liberty first, identitarians put identity first. Just to be clear, I am using "identitarian" in a broad generic sense. There can be identitarians of all races. There can also be identitarians of all nations and ethnic groups. I am not speaking specifically about the Identitarian Movement in

---

* This is a heavily edited and expanded transcript of an extemporaneous talk delivered at the Northwest Forum in Seattle on June 9, 2018. I want to thank the organizers, the audience, and James B. for the transcription.

Europe, although it is an example of white identity politics.

White identity politics inevitably takes different forms in different white societies. The French are different from the Poles, so French identitarianism will be different from Polish identitarianism. But all forms of white identity politics will have some things in common. As an American, my primary focus is the United States. But there are lessons here for all white nations facing demographic transformation due to non-white immigration. There are also lessons for non-white nations facing similar threats.

White identity politics requires more than simple awareness of group identity, group differences, and group conflicts. Whites must also be willing to *defend* our interests whenever they conflict with the interests of other groups. White identity politics means that whites are going to collectivize, organize, and take our own side in the political realm.

The biggest political taboo today is against white identity politics. This is true throughout the Anglosphere and Western Europe. This taboo is the dividing line between identitarians and the rest of the political spectrum. The center-Right wants to draw the line there, and everybody to their Left draws the line there as well.

If you organize as a white person for white people, if you speak as a white person for the interests of white people, and especially if you're willing to act in the political realm for the interests of white people, that is crossing the line into thoughtcrime. It's us versus the whole political system.

Basic Distinctions

We need to make a few distinctions when we talk about identity politics.

The first distinction is between *explicit* and *implicit*

white identity politics. Explicit white identity politics is openly standing up for white interests. Implicit white identity politics is not openly standing up for white interests but "just so happening" to support policies that resonate more with white people than with anybody else.

Basically every center-Right mainstream party in the white world is practicing implicit white identity politics. And a lot of Left-wing politics is also implicit white identity politics. The Bernie Sanders movement promoting Scandinavian-style socialism in America and the Green Parties throughout the white world are forms of implicit white identity politics. Only white people really care about these issues. It's just a different kind of white identity politics.

Implicit white identity politics is ultimately based upon biology. As living things, we are wired to feel more comfortable around people who are genetically similar to us. J. Philippe Rushton was an evolutionary psychologist who developed what is called Genetic Similarity Theory and applied it to the argument for nationalism.[1] Rushton argued that science proves that harmonious relations between individuals are strongly correlated with genetic similarity. Increasing genetic similarity leads to increasing harmony. Increasing genetic diversity leads to increasing conflict. Since harmony strengthens and conflicts weaken a society, genetic similarity is a source of strength, and genetic diversity is a source of weakness.

We know this from looking at the most striking cases of genetic similarity, namely identical twins. Identical twins have the most harmonious relationships among human beings because they are genetically the same. This means they can basically read one another's minds

---

[1] J. P. Rushton, "Ethnic Nationalism, Evolutionary Psychology, and Genetic Similarity Theory," *Nations and Nationalism* 11 (2005): 489–507.

and complete one another's sentences. I met a pair of identical twins years ago, and one of them said, "We're not so much two people as we're one egg divided." I thought that was a beautiful expression. "One egg divided" would be a great title for a book on identical twins.[2]

White people should start thinking of ourselves that way. We're not so much individuals; we're one race divided. We're one race divided up into individuals, peoples, and states. But we're part of one great genetic continuum, going all the way back to the Ice Age and before. If you have that sense of extended family, of unity, of community—it's only natural that you're going to start gravitating towards people who are like you.

Implicit white identity politics, as practiced by conservative parties, is basically a swindle. They will "dog whistle" to us, meaning that they will signal in an oblique way that they understand our racial anxieties. They will propose universalistic legislation that "just so happens" to coincide with our interests as white people. But they'll never *explicitly* court us. Indeed, if you accuse them of being interested in preserving the white race, they will angrily denounce you. They will do anything to avoid the stigma of standing up for their own people.

I used to think that conservatives are unprincipled, but that's not really true. Unfortunately, they are very principled. The trouble is that the principles they hold most sacred are provided by our enemies: namely, identity politics is wrong if practiced by whites but okay for non-whites; racism is bad when practiced by whites, but okay when practiced against us. The entire political mainstream treats this monstrous double standard as sacrosanct. If conservatives act on those principles, they

---

[2] Nancy Segal, *Born Together—Reared Apart: The Landmark Minnesota Twin Study* (Cambridge: Harvard University Press, 2012).

can only lose, and if we depend on them, we can only be destroyed.

White identity politics is quite a broad phenomenon if it can include Republicans dog-whistling to white voters all the way to self-described White Nationalists like me.

Another distinction we need to make within white identity politics is between *white separatists*, *white supremacists*, and a third category that I am just going to call *uppity white folks*.

I am a *white separatist*, meaning that I want to live in a racially homogeneous society rather than a multiracial society. I want racially homogeneous homelands for all peoples, to the extent that is possible.

White supremacists want whites to rule over other races, which logically presupposes the existence of a multiracial society in which whites are at the top of the hierarchy. If we *must* have multiracial societies, I would want whites and white standards to be supreme. But I recognize that such a society is oppressive to other racial groups, which is why I would prefer separate homelands for all peoples.

White separatists like me are often labeled "white supremacists" by lazy and dishonest journalists who wish to tar us with associations to the Ku Klux Klan. We should insist that they respect our chosen nouns as piously as they respect the chosen pronouns of transsexuals.

Uppity white folks are white people who are content—for now—to live in a multiracial, multicultural society but who are going to take their own side in ethnic conflicts. Uppity white folks are the largest group practicing white identity politics. They tend toward the implicit rather than the explicit end of the spectrum. They tend to be politically moderate. They aren't willing to entertain radical new policies just yet.

But they are starting to notice that diversity simply means white dispossession. They are tired of anti-white propaganda in education and the media. They are tired of anti-white double standards. They recognize that whites have interests that need to be defended. They are frustrated with conservatives who refuse to talk about white identity and white interests. And they are increasingly open to explicit talk of white identity and interests, as long as it is reasonable, moderate, fair to all parties, and not freighted with foreign symbols and ideologies.

Uppity white folks are where white identity politics is growing. They are the people we can agitate and radicalize. The Left thinks that the tens of millions of white people who voted for Donald Trump are uppity white folks. That's an exaggeration, of course. But the Trump electorate is definitely our target audience.

White Identity Politics Is Inevitable

White identity politics is inevitable because of multiculturalism. Multiculturalism means many different races and cultures living within the same system, occupying the same public spaces, accessing the same services, trying to determine the direction of policy. It's a battle between groups for control of the state apparatus.

There is no such thing as a *common good* in a multicultural society, because there is no single people. There are many peoples competing for control over a single state, a single economy, and a single set of resources. Once white people see their interests being threatened, it is inevitable that we will start organizing to preserve and advance our interests.

To draw this conclusion, we don't need to know anything about morality or Genetic Similarity Theory or the dynamics of multicultural societies. All we need to know is that if you attack someone, he will eventually react. If you push white people around long enough, we are going to push back.

"Diversity" is just a euphemism for fewer white people. Why would any sane white person celebrate that? As soon as white people recognize that fact, a reaction is inevitable. We are that reaction. And the trajectory of that reaction is to move from implicit white identity politics to explicit white identity politics.

White Identity Politics is Necessary

White identity politics is necessary. More precisely, *explicit* white identity politics is necessary. Why do we have to go explicit? A lot of people don't want to explicitly advocate for white interests. They want to be civic nationalists, Trumpian populists, or Western chauvinists.

If you get such people in a quiet room and pour some liquor into them, they'll assure us that they're totally "based" and really on the side of explicit white identitarians. But then they will explain why they think openly standing up for white people is a dumb strategy. Our enemies will call us racists. Our cucky friends will disavow us. We might actually lose the support of white people.

But if we soft-peddle appeals to white interests and instead uphold the universal principles of "Americanism," we'll keep white supporters—because they can always be taken for granted—and maybe we can split off 10% of the black vote! We can get Kanye West to save our race! And the beauty of it is, we don't even need to talk about what we're doing. We can overthrow the system while not endangering our place in it. Isn't that clever?

In the short run, it seems like a clever gambit. The trouble is that in the long run, it dooms us. Here is why if we don't go explicit, we're doomed.

Imagine American politics as a poker game. In this game, every group in our society—every racial group, every ethnic group—has a seat at the table and a stack of chips. Whites are the largest group in the society, so we've got the biggest stack of chips. But the way the game is played is that every other group has a wild card, namely the "race card," the "identity card," but white people don't.

We cannot play the identity card. We have to say, "This policy is for the good of all humanity, and it just so happens to be good for us." And, of course, if people point out, "Well, it really just seems to be better for you than for other people," you are forced into a choice. You can either say, "Yeah, so what? We're going to take our own side. We want to win this round." But that is to play the identity card. And if you are not willing to do that, you have to back off. You have to cuck. You have to give in.

If you play by those rules long enough—when they can play the "race card" and you can't—you are going to lose. You would never consent to playing a game of poker where every other person at the table gets to use a wild card, but you don't. By those rules, no matter how many advantages you have at the start of the game, every hand you play is going to put you closer and closer to losing it all. The only way not to lose that game is not to play it.

The way to stop playing that game is to give up the ridiculous taboo against white identity politics. White people simply need to say, "We represent the interests of white people. We built the country. We made it great. It's our only homeland, and we're not going to allow it to be taken away from us. We're not going to be diddled out of a homeland by playing by these rigged rules."

Of course the cucks will say that we should never give in to identity politics. We should just try to persuade all the other groups in society to stop engaging in identity politics. But why would any sane group of people voluntarily stop using a winning strategy? Why would any group exchange a winning strategy for a losing one? Will they do it if the losers ask nicely? We see how well that works for Republicans.

So in terms of long-term survival, we have to go explicit. But Republicans only think in terms of the short run. Because white identity politics is a taboo they will never break, they will not deal forthrightly with the anti-white demographic trends baked into the system today, which if unchecked will destroy their party. Non-whites vote more than 70% for the Democrats, and the high immigration and fertility of non-whites means they will be the majority in less than a generation, unless we reverse those demographic trends.

The short-term consequence of breaking the taboo on white identity politics is being called names by journalists. The long-term consequences are a Democratic one-party state and the destruction of everything that conservatives want to conserve. Intelligent and responsible people think about the long run. Foolish, irresponsible people think only about the short run. Strong people are willing to put up with short-term pains for long-term gains. Weak people are not. Republicans are weak, foolish, and irresponsible people. They are letting the Left drag this country into the abyss and cement their power with a one-party state.

Republicans evade thinking about the demographic Armageddon facing their party by fervently believing in the myth of the "based" black or mestizo in a Trump hat. Maybe Diamond and Silk will save them. Maybe Kanye will miracle them into the White House or the Senate one more time. But, as I said to a Tea Party woman more than a decade ago, "There aren't enough fiscally conservative black people in the world to save you." I knew exactly how many black people supported the Tea Party, because they were always on the platform at any event. That's not enough to save them. As the old joke goes, "What do you call the single black man at a Republican event? The keynote speaker." This foolishness is destroying America.

That's why explicit white identity politics is not just inevitable, it is necessary. We must go explicit; we must buck the taboos; we must deal with the long-term problem of white demographic decline. Or we will see all that we love destroyed by a Democratic one-party state ruling over an America that increasingly resembles Mexico or Brazil.[3]

For center-Right politicians, the long-term is measured in decades. But truly long-term arguments for white identity politics look ahead centuries. If we don't change course, center-Right parties will be extinct within a few decades. In my book *The White Nationalist Manifesto*, I argue that that if we don't change course, the entire white race will be extinct within a few centuries, simply because of bad political decisions. Reversing those decisions to secure our race's long-term survival is the essence of white identity politics.[4]

White Identity Politics is Moral

The biggest question that we must deal with before people are going to accept white identity politics is not whether it is *inevitable* or whether it is *necessary* but whether it is *right*. People will refuse to bow to the inevitable if they think that's the *wrong* thing to do. They will refuse to do what is necessary if they think that's the *wrong* thing to do.

---

[3] For more arguments for the necessity of white identity politics, see Greg Johnson, "In the Short Run," *The White Nationalist Manifesto*, second ed. (San Francisco: Counter-Currents, 2019) and *It's Okay to Be White: The Best of Greg Johnson* (Hollywood: Ministry of Truth, 2020).

[4] See Greg Johnson, "White Extinction," "White Genocide," and "Ending White Genocide" in *The White Nationalist Manifesto* and *It's Okay to Be White*.

White people are highly conscientious. That's one of our strengths. We don't have to be watched all the time by CCTV cameras to do the right thing. But that is also a great weakness if people can hack our conscientiousness and turn our moral fervor and moral idealism against our interests. That is basically what is driving white dispossession today. So we have to know that white identity politics is moral.

But how does one talk about moral matters? I believe that we must approach this issue with an assumption that can be illustrated with Charlton Heston's story about how he became a Republican. It was 1964, and Barry Goldwater was running for president. Every day Heston passed by a Barry Goldwater billboard. The slogan on the billboard was: "In your heart you know he's right." And, at a certain point, after seeing the billboard day after day, Heston thought "Sonofabitch! He is right!," and he was converted.[5]

My underlying assumption, whenever I speak to people about moral issues, is that *in their hearts, they know we're right*, because they're wired the same way as we're wired. They are wired to have in-group preferences, to be more comfortable around people who are more similar to them, to be less comfortable around people who are more different. Those are their true feelings. They might have a lot of high-minded liberal, globalist ideas clouding their judgment, but that nonsense doesn't sit well with their own instincts.

That means that in every white Leftist, in every white globalist, we have a fifth column: their own ethnocentric instincts. That's an ally in them to which we can appeal. We can say to them: "Look, you're lying to yourself; you're fooling yourself. You say that you just *love* diversi-

---

[5] Charlton Heston, *In the Arena* (New York: Simon & Schuster, 1995).

ty. But your behavior patterns don't indicate that." As Joe Sobran once observed, "In their mating and migratory habits, liberals are indistinguishable from members of the Ku Klux Klan."[6]

Thus white liberals are constantly fighting against themselves. They feel they must profess a certain creed to be decent, and yet that creed is profoundly alien to their deeper instincts. Thus we can appeal to the fact that, on some level, they already agree with us.

How can we make our people aware of their tacit ethnocentrism? Through Socratic discussion we can get them to reflect on what they really feel. We can also display the contradictions and absurd consequences of the globalist universalist ideology that pits them against us and against their own better natures.

There are many different ethical theories. Some of them use intimidating technical vocabularies and complex arguments. But you do not need to surrender your ethical judgment to experts, because all these theories are just attempts to articulate what we all know, in our hearts, to be right.

Knowing what is right is not, however, the same as *saying* what is right. We always know more than we can say. So any attempt to say what is right will actually fall short of what we know. Which means that all ethical theories fall more or less short of the truth.

For instance, when someone says that the good is the same thing as pleasure—a theory known as hedonism—we all know that is untrue. Why? Because if pleasure is the good, there can be no bad pleasures or good pains. But we can all think of examples of bad pleasures and good pains. Nicotine addiction is a bad pleasure. Nicotine withdrawal is a good pain.

---

[6] Jared Taylor, "Jared Taylor Remembers Joe Sobran," *VDare*, October 1, 2010.

If someone says that justice is simply respecting people's property rights, we know that is untrue, because if a friend loaned you his gun, then demanded it back in order to commit a crime, it would not be just to return it.

If someone says that justice is simply a matter of helping your friends and harming your enemies, we know that is untrue, because sometimes our friends do the wrong thing, and sometimes our enemies do the right thing.

Every moral theory, therefore, is merely a more or less adequate attempt to say what we all know, in our hearts, is right. Because of that, even though in our hearts we know the *same* things, we inevitably *say* different things when we talk about the good. Which means that we disagree about right and wrong.

But the only way to overcome these disagreements is to *say more*, to *talk our differences through*. In conversation, we can test our partial and inadequate opinions about the good and replace them with broader, more adequate accounts. This process could continue forever, but generally we call it quits when we arrive at a consensus whose unity mirrors the unity of what we already know, even though we despair of ever fully saying it.

Love of One's Own

One of the foundational questions about identity politics is the morality of ingroup preference, i.e., love of one's own.

Is there anything wrong with people preferring their own children to their neighbors' children? If your father said to you, "We have learned that the neighbor boy has much better grades than you, so we're going send him to college instead of you," I think most people would recognize that your dad is a monster. There is something unnatural about preferring other people's children to your own. Your father would have to be mentally addled by some kind of universalist ideology before he would say something like that. But the underlying problem has to be a lack of normal human sentiment.

It is natural, normal, and right to love one's own, to take care of one's own, and to give them precedence over strangers. People who lack these sentiments are monsters, and we should not be looking to them for moral advice or examples.

It is also natural, normal, and right to prefer your friends to strangers, your hometown to other towns, your homeland over foreign lands, your nation over other nations, and your race over other races. Even if you were raised by wolves in a warzone, you would still be tethered to them by such sentiments.

There are historical, cultural, and ultimately biological reasons for these preferences. It is natural to feel a stronger connection to people who share the same historical experiences, for instance, members of one's own generation as opposed to older and younger generations. It is also natural to feel a stronger connection to people who share the same language and customs, because one can understand and cooperate with them more easily.

But the deepest reasons for these preferences are biological. Genetic Similarity Theory predicts that you will have more harmonious relationships, and a greater tendency toward feelings of solidarity and altruism, with people who are genetically similar.

Is love of one's own a "selfish" sentiment? Yes and no. Our genes are very selfish. They want to propagate themselves through time. However, because our genes are present in other people, they can better propagate themselves if those who share the same genes cooperate with one another, are kind to one another, take risks for one another, and even die for one another. The more genes people share in common, the more solidarity, cooperation, and altruism they display among each other. Our selfish genes program us for altruism.

Thus it follows that the most unselfish and public-spirited societies are those with the least genetic diversity. The claim that "All men are brothers" aims to foster cooperation, solidarity, and altruism based on an implicit understanding of genetic similarity. But it is not literally true. One cannot have a society in which all men are brothers. But one can have societies in which all men are cousins. And it turns out that some of the happiest societies in the world—Denmark, Iceland—are among the genetically most homogeneous, where all people basically are cousins or their genetic equivalents.[7]

If it is natural, normal, and right to prefer people who are like you, then we have to conclude that the flip side of loving one's own—namely, discomfort around those who are different, i.e., xenophobia—is also natural, normal, and right.

Thus we have to conclude that there is something perverse about people who prefer the foreign and exotic over the familiar. The bigger the plate in their lip, the more fascinating they become. The term for this is *xenophilia.*

We have pious Christians who lecture us on the duty of loving our neighbors. But how do they love their neighbors? By inflicting Somali Muslim migrants on them. But this is not loving their neighbors; it is betraying them. Xenophilia is a perversion of natural moral sentiments, which disguises itself as a devotion to high principles. It is a highly selfish form of moral fanaticism and exhibitionism, and we simply need to call these peo-

---

[7] Marie Helweg-Larsen, "Why Denmark Is the Happiest Country," *Live Science*, March 30, 2018; Genetics Society of America, "Genomic Study of High School Students from Across Denmark Reveals Remarkable Genetic Homogeneity," *Science Daily*, October 11, 2016.

ple out on it. These people are as monstrous as the father who prefers the neighbor kid to his own. Again, this is a perversion of natural moral sentiments cloaking itself as high moral principle.

If love of one's own is natural, normal, and right, then white identity politics is natural, normal, and right. Identity politics is simply the politics of loving one's own.

Self-Actualization

One of the most compelling moral theories is that the good life is one of self-actualization: of becoming who you are.

But we all know that self-actualization is not a complete account of the good life, because we can distinguish between potentialities that are good, bad, and not necessarily good or bad. Thus self-actualization is not necessarily a good thing, and stifling self-actualization is not necessarily a bad thing. After all, humans have a lot of potentialities, and if self-actualization were simply the same as the good life, then actualization of *all* these potentialities would be good.

But we all recognize there are bad potentialities, for instance, vices. We all have the potential to be lazy, greedy, or imprudent. We all recognize that there are bad seeds. Would a good society allow Jeffrey Dahmer or Hannibal Lecter to actualize himself? Even Aristotle, who is known as the great advocate of self-actualization, only praises self-actualization *in accordance with virtue*, i.e., *good* self-actualization.[8]

We also recognize that it is not necessarily good or bad if one takes up golf or fishing, piano or clarinet, needlepoint or quilting, yet all of these choices involve actu-

---

[8] Aristotle states that *eudaimonia* (happiness, well-being, living well) is "actuality of the soul in accordance with virtue" in *Nicomachean Ethics* 1098a16.

alizing various potentialities.

So there is more to goodness than self-actualization. But still, we need to actualize our potentialities for virtue. Beyond that, it makes sense to say that *happiness* is a matter of actualizing one's individuality. Potentialities that are not necessarily good or bad *in themselves* may still be good or bad *for you*.

Since we are all individuals, you might be better suited for golf than fishing, for piano than clarinet, for intellectual work rather than hard labor, for solitude rather than society, etc. Just as we are more comfortable in shoes and clothes that fit our bodies and the climate, we are more comfortable and more alive when we choose activities that go with rather than against our natures.

Thus we can say that the purpose of life is to actualize our *best* potentialities, to become the *best* versions of ourselves. After all, we cannot be anyone else. We can only be ourselves. But we do have a choice of being self-actualized or frustrated, happy or miserable versions of ourselves.

Self-actualization is not just for individuals. It also makes sense to talk about *collective* self-actualization. Every human being has two identities: the one given by nature and the other given by society, namely the language, customs, manners, and traditions that we learn from others.

Just as some forms of life are consistent with one's individual identity and others conflict with it, some forms of life express one's cultural identity and others conflict with it. When a people is free to express its collective identity, it stamps its identity on the public realm. It expresses its identity in the dates it honors, in the monuments it erects, in the names it gives to its cities and streets, in the language of government, etc.

When a people expresses its collective identity in public, it creates a homeland. A homeland is not just a place on the map. It is a realm of shared meaning, in which people understand one another, feel comfortable with one another, and can live, work, play, and celebrate with one another.

This is why multiculturalism cannot really work. Cultures with opposed conventions cannot exist comfortably in the same system. To choose a trivial example, the American and British systems of driving cannot exist in the same country. Or, to choose a far less trivial example, European and Muslim sexual mores cannot exist in the same society. Trying to force different cultures into the same space causes collisions and conflicts. Multicultural societies basically force you to either fight constantly with other groups about conflicting values and customs, or to stop caring about them, so you don't fight.

Americans have been sold the tale that we are "a nation of immigrants," a phrase made famous when Senator John F. Kennedy used it as the title of the book he wrote for the Antidefamation League of B'nai B'rith.[9] Americans believe that we have a long and successful history of assimilating different European ethnic groups into a common American identity.

So we are told that it is un-American to oppose immigration, even though we never successfully assimilated non-white groups, and even though we have stopped even *trying* to assimilate immigrants. We are multiculturalists now, which means the abandonment of assimilation.

But assimilationism was no picnic either. If you look at American history, the assimilation of even closely related European peoples was accompanied by a great deal of conflict, turmoil, and bloodshed. And in the end, assimilation often did not take the form of newcomers adopting the dominant way of life. Instead, assimilation

---

[9] John F. Kennedy, *A Nation of Immigrants* (New York: Harper & Row, 1964).

meant that all parties simply ceased caring about the things that divided them, things that their ancestors had cared about intensely.

America was an overwhelmingly Protestant nation from its founding. But the conflicts that ensued when millions of Catholics immigrated to America, first from Ireland then from places like Poland and Italy, did not lead to the conversion of Catholics to Protestantism, or to a higher synthesis of Protestantism and Catholicism. Instead, to avoid conflicts, many Americans simply stopped caring about something that used to be central to the identity of the nation.

Now, I must hasten to add that I don't care about religion. I am glad Americans are less divided by narrow sectarian Christian conflicts. I am glad Christianity doesn't matter enough for people to fight and die over it anymore. But I also recognize that Protestantism was an integral part of the society that my ancestors struggled to build and bequeath to me, and that we who abandoned that legacy proved ourselves unworthy heirs.

Different ethnic groups are real. White Americans constitute a distinct people. If we are going to be ourselves, we can no longer abandon the public realm to multicultural chaos and retreat into private life. Multiculturalism creates a society in which everyone feels alien. That's no way to live.

We have a right to a land where we feel at home, where we are comfortable, where public transportation is safe, where children can play without supervision, where we can understand and trust strangers because, in the end, they're not all that strange. So, from the point of view of collective self-actualization, we need to own up to our ethnic identities and ethnocentric preferences. Then we need to create ethnically homogeneous homelands where we are free to be ourselves. In short, white self-actualization requires white identity politics.

Universalizability

Love of one's own and self-actualization are all about the unique, individual, and particular: what differentiates individuals from individuals and peoples from peoples.

But the idea that true moral principles are *universal* has a great deal of intuitive appeal. If something is *true*, that means it is *true for everyone*. If something is *right*, that means it is *right for everyone*. Immanuel Kant argued that a principle is not moral unless you can will it to be a universal law.

But there is nothing un-universalizable about the principle that you take care of your own first, and you let other people take care of their own first. There is nothing un-universalizable about the principle of individuals and groups actualizing their unique potentials for excellence and letting other individuals and groups do the same. We can all live quite contentedly under such rules, and in fact they actually forward the good much better than the alternative.

What is the alternative? What does it mean to say that it is *not* right to take care of the people who are nearest and dearest to us first? Are we assuming that other people are going to take care of them? Why would other people take care of people that they *don't* have much connection to? It just doesn't make any sense.

If you want to live in a world where everybody gets some consideration, it is best to do what comes naturally, i.e., take care of the ones who are genetically closest to us, our kin. And, if you follow that rule in your life, that does not impede anybody else from following the same rule, and in fact, you have a better world for doing so.

We also have to question the idea that if something is good, it is good for everyone. There is an ambiguity in the phrase "for everyone." Let's grant that some moral principles are true for everyone. Principles like "Promote the good; spurn the evil," are surely true for everyone, meaning that everyone should follow them.

But are all questions of what is good, right, or fitting equally universal? To choose a trivial example, it might be the case that size twelve shoes are right for my feet. As an objective fact about my feet, that is true for everybody. But that does not imply that everybody has size twelve feet or should wear size twelve shoes.

When we talk about basic moral principles, one size might fit all people. But when we talk about self-actualization—individual and collective—then there are no one-size-fits-all solutions. Different ways of life are fitting for different people. But that is still an objective fact, and the principle that everyone should actualize his unique potentialities for excellence is entirely universalizable.

Another way to approach this is to distinguish between moral *relativism* and moral *subjectivism*. Relativism is the idea that what is good, right, or fitting varies between times, places, and individuals. When one asks, "What is right?" the answer is: "That depends"—on time, place, and individuality, so there is no single right answer. *Subjectivism* is the idea that what is good, right, etc. depends entirely on our subjective feelings and decisions.

Every subjectivist is a relativist, because he believes that the good depends on his subjectivity. But not every relativist is a subjectivist. One can be an *objective* relativist. It is an objective fact that size twelve shoes are the best fit for size twelve feet, but the answer to the question "What is the best shoe size?" is "Depends on the foot."

Identity politics claims that the best way of life depends on the unique identities of peoples. It does not deny that there are some moral and political universals. But those are not enough for a good society. There is no universal language. There is no universal culture. There is no universal mythology, costume, or cuisine. Universalistic ideologies like liberalism, however, claim that, beyond universal moral and political principles, there is one best way of life for all peoples. Identity politics is the custom-tailored suit. One-worldism is the equivalent of forcing everyone to wear flip-flops and Maoist boiler suits. But just because identity politics focuses on the particular, that does not mean it isn't good for everyone, since every individual and every people has its own particularities.

FAIRNESS

Another intuitively plausible moral principle is "fairness." Even little kids understand fairness. You constantly hear them saying "No fair!," especially during games and meals.

Fairness is connected with universalizability. For instance, the "Golden Rule" bids us to "Do unto others as you would have others do unto you." In other words, what is good for you is also good for others.

When John Locke talks about appropriating things from nature—making something your own—he said that fairness requires us to leave "as much and as good" for others. So, if you're the first guy on the island, and you plant your flag and say, "It's all mine!," the people coming up the beach behind you might say, "Wait a second here, you need to leave some for us too."

John Rawls' idea of "justice as fairness" urges people to design a social order in which we could morally accept trading places with any other person. There can be many different stations, roles, and ways of life in such a society. But none of them should be morally outrageous, like being a slave or being forced to sell your organs for survival.

Fairness means, *in some sense*, not treating others fundamentally differently than you treat yourself. But identity politics is all about doing justice to our differences. So we must ask: Is white identity politics fair?

There is nothing unfair about ethnonationalism. The ethnonationalist says: "I'm going to take care of those who are closest to me first, and I'm going to accept that other people will do the same thing. I'm going to create a homeland where my language, traditions, and way of life are normative, and where my extended family can flourish, and I will accept the desire of others to do the same. I'm going to accept that if I'm a stranger in a foreign land, the natives come first; their comfort comes before my comfort. I want to live by those rules in my country, and I'm willing to live by those rules in countries where I travel."

The basic Identitarian principle is to plant one's flag and say, "This country is this ours; this is our homeland; invaders and colonists must leave." There is nothing unfair about that, because the invaders and colonists have homelands of their own.

But the current situation, in which whites—and *only* whites—are being asked to accept replacement levels of immigration from the Third World, while Third Worlders keep their homelands, is totally unfair. What's theirs, they keep. What's ours is negotiable. That's a morally outrageous proposition. Repatriating invaders and colonists is not, however, unfair, because at the end of the process, everyone has a homeland.

There are good and bad kinds of nationalism. Bad nationalists seek to secure the sovereignty of their own people, but they are willing to deny the sovereignty of other peoples. They refuse to treat others the same way they wish to be treated. They defend their own but do not allow others to do the same. They create a world of oppressors and the oppressed, in which they could never risk trading places with others.

Good nationalists believe in nationalism for all nations. They treat other peoples as they would like to be treated themselves. They realize that nobody is immune to misfortune, that oppressor and oppressed can and often do trade places, and that a just world requires abolishing both roles. That kind of white identity politics is not unfair to anyone.

Consequentialism

Moral principles are about governing actions. Actions aim at results. Therefore, it seems plausible that we should justify moral principles by their consequences. A principle is good if it leads to good consequences. It is bad if it leads to bad consequences. This approach to ethics is called "consequentialism." Utilitarianism is one of the best-known forms of consequentialism, which says right actions promote "the greatest good for the greatest number."

It is easy to make a consequentialist argument for white identity politics. In fact, in my book *The White Nationalist Manifesto*, I make precisely that kind of argument. Under the present globalist, multiculturalist, individualist order, all white nations are in demographic decline. If this decline is not reversed, whites will cease to exist as a distinct race. What would reverse these alarming demographic trends? We don't need to go into detail here. Suffice it to say that governments would have to make white preservation and flourishing the overriding goal of public policy. In short, they would have to adopt some form of white identity politics.

White extinction would not have negative consequences for whites alone. Nonwhites would suffer, as would the planet as a whole. As Charles Murray exhaustively documents in his book *Human Accomplishment*, whites are by far the most creative race.[10] White people

---

[10] Charles Murray, *Human Accomplishment: The Pursuit of*

have created great cities, great civilizations, great languages, great art, and enormous chunks of what we think of as science, technology, and modernity. Many non-whites around the world genuinely admire and eagerly benefit from white achievements. They would mourn our passing.

Of course, some of our past achievements would continue to exist even if whites went extinct, but we would have no future achievements. The world, however, is facing enormous challenges to sustain both human life and the planet as a whole as exploding populations use up finite resources. The only way to save mankind, and the planet, from such a Malthusian crisis is technological innovation, which is still disproportionately a white thing. White technological achievement, however, requires white preservation, which requires white identity politics.[11] If we want to save the world, we have to save the whites, thus white identity politics truly produces the greatest good for the greatest number.

WILL WE WIN?

I have argued that white identity politics is inevitable, that it is necessary, and that it is moral. Which brings us to the final question: Will we win? That brings us to the big problem with consequentialism. We can't really predict and control all the consequences of our actions.

Victory depends on two kinds of things: things we can control and things we can't. The things that we can't control are basically the historical conditions in which we operate. If conditions are not right, then no matter

---

Excellence in the Arts and Sciences, 800 B.C. to 1950 (New York: HarperCollins, 2003).

[11] Greg Johnson, "Technological Utopianism and Ethnic Nationalism," in *Toward a New Nationalism* (San Francisco: Counter-Currents, 2019) and *It's Okay to Be White.*

how well organized we are, we cannot win. If conditions are right, but we are not ready for them, then we can't win either.

So we have to focus on what we can control. We need to be the best possible versions of ourselves, both as individuals and as a community. We need to become a ruling elite in waiting. To do that, we must aim at attracting intelligent, enterprising people and encourage them to acquire educations, build networks, amass wealth, found institutions, and start dynasties.

Then, if historical events start breaking in our favor, we can actually stop having history done to us and start making history again. And if conditions never break in our favor, we can console ourselves with the fact that we will still be a formidable community—the *white people with a future*—even if we can't secure a future for all white people.

To sustain ourselves in this struggle, we need to keep two ideas in mind.

First, even though it is not in our power to foresee and control all consequences, it is in our power to act on the right principles and to cultivate excellence. Therefore, we need to follow the ancient Aryan ethos that is found in the Bhagavad Gita, the Stoics, and Kant: Do the right thing, and let the gods sort out the rest. Thus, even if we don't win, we can console ourselves with the knowledge that *we at least deserved to win*.

Second, there is good reason to hope that we will win, because our ideas are in harmony with reality and because it really is true of all our people—even our most stubborn enemies—that in their hearts, they know we're right.

Counter-Currents, August 30, 2019;
February 20, 2020; February 25, 2020

THREE PILLARS OF WHITE IDENTITY POLITICS:
KINSHIP, CULTURE, LOVE OF ONE'S OWN*

"THIS IS WHO WE ARE"

When you look at human history, identity politics is not the exception, it is the norm. History is the story of us and them: tribes, city-states, and nations trading with and fighting against one another. If you look at the members of any of these groups, you will find that they are united by ties of kinship, a common language and culture, a common history and sense of destiny, and bonds of fellow feeling.

Of course, all other groups have these traits as well. But those people belong to *different* kinship groups; they are bound by *different* languages and customs; they have *different* histories and destinies; moreover, their bonds of fellow feeling don't extend to their neighbors, who might well be enemies.

The power of the state can touch every aspect of life. Thus anything can become the topic of political debate. Political debates can appeal to many kinds of arguments: moral, religious, scientific, historical, etc. Identity politics happens whenever the final argument for or against a political proposal comes down to: "This is who we are." This is a statement of identity. We want this law, this institution, this custom, because it *fits* who we are, and a political order should fit the people who live under it as comfortably and flatteringly as a well-tailored suit.

When we appeal to abstract principles and objective

---

* This lecture was written for the Scandza Forum in Zagreb, Croatia, on May 2, 2020. Unfortunately, the event was canceled due to COVID-19.

facts, they are supposed to be true for all of us. But appeals to identity are true for some people but not for others. They are particular, not universal. The politics of identity is also the politics of *difference*, for our identity is precisely what differentiates us from others.

The opposite of identity politics is universalism, which upholds the idea of a single, one-size-fits-all political order based on universally true principles. Universalists claim that identity politics is dangerous because different groups can never reach agreement on political matters if we allow what makes us different to be a final argument. And if different groups can't agree about passionately polarizing political issues, then the only recourse that remains is to fight.

This argument fails for two main reasons.

First, agreement vs. conflict is a false alternative, since two parties can simply agree to disagree. But agreeing to disagree only works if the different parties really don't care all that much about the issue that divides them. If they care a great deal, however, then they can't agree to disagree, since only one position can actually prevail. For instance, abortion is either legal or illegal, which means that the only alternative to fighting is for one side to bow to the will of the other.

But this brings us to the second problem in the universalist argument. Abortion cannot be both legal and illegal *in the same state*, but it can be both legal in one state and illegal in another. In short, there is an alternative to fighting when two groups have passionate and irreconcilable differences about political issues: They can go their separate ways.

Abortion is a single political issue, but people feel passionate enough about it to shed blood. The clashes between different peoples are far more complex, involving language, religion, culture, whole ways of life. Thus their potential for deep polarization and explosive violence is far greater, as is the need for political separation.

This is why I argue that ethnonationalism is the best system for handling the politics of identity. Ethnonationalism upholds the right of all peoples to sovereign homelands if they feel their identities are threatened in multicultural, multiracial societies.

Note that a right is an *option*, not an *obligation*. If a people is content in a multicultural society, it is not obligated to break away. But if it chooses to exercise its right, then heaven and earth have no right to stop them.

Multicultural societies are, however, prone to conflict around issues of identity. There are two ways to handle these conflicts. First, in order to decrease social frictions, different peoples can simply *cease caring* about the things that separate them. This, however, only works if their differences are trivial to begin with. But what if they differ on important matters?

This brings us to the second option: to fight. When fighting about important differences starts, there are only two ways to end such conflicts permanently: the utter destruction of one group or political separation and the creation of new sovereign states. Separation is the best option because it ends the violence and erosion of identities endemic to multicultural societies, giving all parties the chance to flourish in their own homelands, where "This is who we are" can go unchallenged.

Of course "who we are" is not always good. Sometimes aspects of identity are bad. Peoples cling to alcoholism, imperialism, and the worst sorts of superstition because of appeals to identity. Some peoples are afflicted with genetic disorders that they should not want to afflict on their posterity. Every people can be improved. Moreover, it is entirely natural, normal, and right for peoples to want to improve themselves: to hand on a better society—and better genes—to future generations.

Ethnonationalism, however, lets different peoples work

out their own problems. We reject progressive and paternalistic arguments for ruling over other peoples. "This is who we are" always trumps "It's for your own good," even if it really is for their own good, since the greater good is to create peace between different peoples and let them wrestle with their own demons.

Separating hostile peoples can be accomplished through moving borders and moving people. In practice, it usually involves some combination of the two. Separation can be accomplished peacefully, as in the "velvet divorce" between the Czechs and the Slovaks, or through terror and violence, as in the breakup of Yugoslavia. The results are the same, but the violent path is far more costly. Since the goal of ethnonationalism is creating peace between different peoples, we naturally prefer to achieve it by peaceful means as well.

It has been known since ancient times that the tripod is the most stable foundation. Identity politics rests on an unwobbling tripod, three facts about human nature that make identity politics inevitable and ethnonationalism preferable: kinship, culture, and love of one's own.

Kinship

The first pillar of identity politics is kinship. In connecting kinship and identity politics, I follow the arguments of J. Philippe Rushton and Frank Salter.[1]

Politics aims at living well together in society. The more amicable, cooperative, and trustworthy the people are, the more harmonious the society. The more willing the people are to come together and make sacrifices for

---

[1] J. P. Rushton, "Ethnic Nationalism, Evolutionary Psychology, and Genetic Similarity Theory," *Nations and Nationalism* 11 (2005): 489–507 and Frank Salter, *On Genetic Interests: Family, Ethnicity, & Humanity in an Age of Mass Migration* (New Brunswick, N.J.: Transaction Publishers, 2006).

the common good, especially in times of disaster and war, the more likely the society is to survive and bounce back.

The root of pro-social behavior is *empathy*, meaning the ability to *see oneself in others*. The expression of pro-social empathy is *altruism*, meaning treating the interests of others as equal to—or even more important than—one's own. I am going to refer to empathy and altruism simply as *pro-social virtues*. The result of pro-social virtues is social harmony and well-being.

There is a strong correlation between kinship and pro-social behaviors, ranging from fellow-feeling to willingness to sacrifice one's interests and even one's life for the common good.

But the connection between kinship and pro-social virtues is problematic. Kinship, after all, means sharing the same genes. Genes, however, are notoriously "selfish." They aim at their propagation into the next generation. Since individual organisms are the carriers of genes, wouldn't individuals be selfish as well? How, then, is altruism anything other than a biological disadvantage, a kind of handicap or morbidity?

The answer is that the individual is not the only carrier of his genes. His genes are also present in other people. The closer the kinship, the more genes we have in common. The closer the kinship, the greater the empathy, for we can *literally* see more of ourselves in our kin. Thus we would expect more altruistic behavior directed toward closer kin. This is why, from a selfish gene's point of view, it makes sense for an individual to die for his family and his tribe, since they contain more of his selfish genes than he does.

Thus we would expect greater social harmony and well-being in societies that are more genetically homogeneous, and less harmony and well-being in more genetically diverse societies. This fact alone refutes the modern dogma that genetic diversity strengthens societies.

Until the twentieth century, it was universally acknowledged that kinship is the foundation of politics. The very concepts of "nation" and "ethnicity" are etymologically derived from concepts for kinship. Even today, the primary way that people become citizens of any political order is being born that way, meaning that they are kin to those who are already citizens. Even globalists acknowledge the importance of kinship by declaring that "All men are brothers," therefore, we should have no borders and no countries, just a global market and a global state, because common blood trumps everything that sets us apart.

But not all men are brothers. Your brother has the same parents as you do, which means that you both arise from the same set of genes, although mixed in different ways. Unless, of course, you have an identical twin brother, in which case you have the exact same genes.

So not all men are brothers. But as far as we know, all human beings descend from common pre-human ancestors. Thus we are all more or less distant cousins. But the distances between the great continental races and subraces—whites, blacks, Asians, Amerindians, non-European Caucasians, Australoids, and Capoids—are significant enough that radically different forms of societies suit them, which means that societies with multiple races suffer from conflicts that do not afflict racially homogeneous societies.

This is why some globalists declare that we will have a stable global society only when all racial and cultural differences have been erased. In short, some globalists are ethnonationalists. They believe in the "one people, one nation" principle. Thus to construct a single world state, they wish to construct a single, mongrelized humanity. So much for diversity.

Ethnonationalists also believe in "one people, one state" (at *least* one state per people), but instead of destroying all existing peoples to create a world state, we wish to preserve all of them by giving them their own sovereign ethnostates.

Does this imply that the natural political unit is the *racial state*, i.e., all whites in one state, all Asians in another? And what do we make of mixed-race people?

Note that I said the first pillar of identity politics is *kinship*. I did not say it is *race*. Race alone is not a sufficient foundation for several reasons.

First, even within races, there are different degrees of relatedness. Genetic diversity, even within a race, may weaken the unity of a society and lead to conflict or the erosion of genetic differences, which are valuable and should be preserved. Note that I have said nothing of cultural diversity within the same races. Culture is the second pillar of identity politics, which we will discuss later.

Second, even societies in which most individuals are of a typical mixed-race type—such as countries in Latin America, the Caribbean, or Southeast Asia—still have an interest in propagating their genes into the future. They are still improved by greater homogeneity and undermined by greater diversity. Race mixing in the past is *never* an argument for increasing diversity in the present. In fact, one reason race-mixing took place in the past is to overcome the problems of diversity, i.e., of multiple races living in the same society.

What, then, is the political utility of the concept of race? Race is first and foremost a *biological* category. How does it become a *political* category?

First, race is politically important because people don't stay in the same place. They migrate to new lands and intermarry with foreigners. Thus the question arises: What are the outer boundaries of assimilability, beyond which foreigners are not good candidates for becoming part of one's society? Race is clearly the outer boundary of assimilability. Thus it made sense for the American founders to limit naturalization to "white persons." Being white is not a *sufficient* condition for being American or German. But it should be a *necessary* condition.

Of course, if a society truly values homogeneity, then mere race is far too expansive a criterion for naturalization, since within the same race there is a great deal of genetic diversity. Beyond that, linguistic, cultural, and religious homogeneity also promote social harmony.

Second, race becomes a political category when Europeans find themselves facing common enemies of other races. When an Irishman and an Englishman spend time together, they tend to focus on their differences. But when they live alongside members of other races, they tend to notice their similarities, especially when there are racial conflicts.

Third, race becomes a political category when Europeans appeal to their common race, as well as deep cultural commonalities, to mediate and mitigate disputes among them.

White Nationalists are fond of the phrase "Our race is our nation." But this is not literally true. The white race is not a people, because peoplehood is more than just kinship, which brings us to the second pillar of white identity politics: culture.

Culture

It is easy to understand why kinship alone is not a sufficient foundation for a harmonious society. Studies of identical twins raised in different environments give remarkable evidence of how fine-grained genetic determinism really is.

But imagine identical twins raised in *really* different environments: one in Yemen, the other in New York City. They might look the same, have the same favorite color, and gravitate toward the same hobbies and careers. But with radically different languages, religions, and value systems, they are hardly interchangeable. They would be completely lost if they switched places, and they would also be more capable of working and living with any random Yemeni or New Yorker than with one another.

In short, culture matters. Biology is our first nature, culture our second nature. Biology provides the hardware of consciousness, culture the software. Both are components of identity, so both matter to identity politics.

Indeed, culture matters so much to identity politics that it frequently trumps considerations of kinship. Thus peoples who are closely related genetically—like the Irish and the English or the Serbs, Croatians, and Bosnians—nurse ancient enmities because of differences of culture. (I include religion in the category of culture.)

A people is not just a group bound together by kinship. They also need to *understand* one another, which means they must share a common language. They also need to share a common history, values, and goals, or they won't work well together. It is also best if they don't belong to competing religious sects that teach people that their neighbors, classmates, and even their own kin are evil and deserve to be tortured for eternity.

In sum, a people is not just a collection of individuals who happen to be related to one another. They also must *think of themselves as a people*. Peoplehood = kinship + a common consciousness. Which means a common culture.

This is why the human race as a whole is not a people. Yes, all men are more or less cousins. But aside from the fact that there are enormous genetic differences between the races, there are enormous cultural chasms as well. We don't share a common language, culture, religion, and way of life. Thus we don't *think* of ourselves as a people.

Of course, there are a few committed cosmopolitans proclaiming the brotherhood of man. But they can't really mean it. They can't understand or relate to the vast majority of the human race. In fact, they can really relate only to fellow cosmopolitans. Beyond that, they feel no real affection for all of mankind. For one thing, they passionately hate nationalists like us. Thus, for the most part, cosmopolitanism is just empty high-minded talk, mere social signaling. But predators also use it as a battering ram to breach the borders of countries they wish to plunder.

If the human race as a whole is not a people, neither is the white race, for the same basic reasons. We may be genetically closer to one another than to the Papuans. But we do not share a common mother language. We have a common culture, but it includes dramatic cultural and religious polarities like Athens versus Jerusalem. We have a common history, but it is largely a record of political division and passionate enmities.

Culture is so prominent in identity politics that it is easy to think that biology plays no role at all. Furthermore, there is such a strong cultural taboo against "racism" that people are tempted to downplay biology or deny it altogether. Maybe we can simply say, "France is for the French. These other people don't belong here." Who needs to say anything about race?

The weakness of a purely cultural approach to identity is that it is too inclusive. It lets in people that the identitarians wish to exclude. If being French is a culture, you don't have to be born French. People can *become* French as well. People migrate and intermarry all the time. Cultural assimilation may be rare and difficult, but it is real. Of course, for an immigrant, French is not his *mother* language. But there are now blacks and Asians for whom French is their mother language. If people from around the globe can become culturally French, then French identitarians have to talk about who are the best candidates for assimilation, which requires that we talk about race.

If one of the necessary conditions of peoplehood is group consciousness, how does this differ from the ideas of civic nationalism and the "social construction" of identity? The simple answer is that real communities require *both* kinship and consciousness.

There are, of course, communities that are pure social constructs, like the Dr. Who Fan Club. But nations, at their core, are kinship groups that share a common consciousness and are dedicated to the tasks of civilized life. That's what makes them stronger, deeper, and more important than fan clubs and other fake identities concocted by consumer culture.

The idea that a nation is a pure social construct means that kinship is not an essential characteristic of nationhood. In concrete terms, that implies that the French people are no longer essential to the enterprise known as France. The French people are replaceable by foreigners, as long as their replacements pay lip-service to the designs of the ruling elite.

Cultural and credal forms of nationalism are organically connected to race replacement. If being American is simply a matter of a culture or a creed, then immigrants who learn English as adults and can pass a civics test are just as American as those who are born and bred to be Americans.

The next step is to argue that they are even *better* Americans. After all, immigrants *choose* to be Americans; they weren't merely born to it, and liberalism makes a fetish of choice. How many Americans who were merely born there could pass a civics test, anyway? And isn't it far easier to learn English as a child than as an adult? Perhaps these lazy, entitled Americans deserve to be replaced by hard-working immigrants, who will be grateful to their employers and to the government who hands them their papers.

When elites define you as replaceable, that's because they intend to replace you. That's why populism is on the rise. The people need to replace the elites before the elites can replace the people.

A real homeland is yours simply by birthright: You belong to it, and it belongs to you. A homeland does not define its citizens as replaceable. Indeed, it defines them as irreplaceable, because its entire purpose is to be their home. A country where you are replaceable is merely an economic zone, and when your borders are open to the clamoring billions of the global South, your days are numbered.

It is interesting that opponents of white identity politics—and *only* white identity politics—think that the idea of the "social construction" of identity is a silver bullet. Social constructivism is really two separate theses: the social construction of *race* and the social construction of *culture*.

I have argued elsewhere that the idea of the social construction of race is baseless and really rather dumb.[2] But even if it were true, it is not an impediment to white identity politics.

First of all, the idea of the social construction of race does not deter the identity politics of non-whites. Indeed, non-white identitarians are often the very people who use the concept against whites. If it does not deter them, why should it deter us?

Whether race is a biological reality or merely a social construct, whites still know who we are (we're the ones who are supposed to bear white guilt), we still have interests, and we can still collectivize to pursue our interests in the political realm. Quibbling about the metaphysical status of whiteness changes nothing from a political point of view.

Second, if race is a social construct, why shouldn't

---

[2] Greg Johnson, "Why Race Is Not a Social Construct," in *In Defense of Prejudice* (San Francisco: Counter-Currents, 2017) and *It's Okay to Be White*.

whites seek to construct whiter nations? Indeed, it would make our task easier, because all questions of who is white can be simply answered by fiat.

Third, there is a sense in which race is shaped by laws and customs, insofar as they institute eugenic and dysgenic breeding policies. For instance, the vast mestizo populations of Latin America came about due to social policies. However, that does not imply that such peoples don't have identities and interests of their own that might lead them to resist further social engineering. Just because they were socially constructed in the past does not mean that they should welcome the designs of elites that wish to transform or replace them.

As for the idea of the social construction of culture: I guess there's nothing society can't construct if it can even construct itself.

There were, of course, animal species (races) before there were cultures. Cultures, therefore, are the "constructs" of various races. Once cultures emerged, however, they influenced the subsequent evolution of races by encouraging dysgenic or eugenic breeding patterns. But races came first.

The amazing variety of cultures within the same race shows, however, that race does not determine every aspect of culture. Biology provides outer boundaries for the range of cultural variations. But within those boundaries, a great deal of culture arises from the free play of the human imagination.

When people speak of culture as a social construct, they mean that cultures are contingent—they didn't have to happen, and they could have been otherwise—and that they persist because they are shared by many people.

To speak of culture as a "construct" or "convention," however, is highly misleading, for these are conscious human creations. People do, of course, create conventions and other social constructs, e.g., red means stop, green means go. But creating such conventions already presupposes a background of other meaningful cultural practices. But if such practices are presupposed by conventions, then they can't themselves be conventions.

Ultimately, language and culture belong to a third category: neither nature, nor convention or construction, but rather *evolved social practices*—products of human action, but not of human design and construction. And if at its core, culture is not a product of human design or construction, then it can't be subjected to wholesale redesign and reconstruction.[3] Changing one's culture is not as simple as changing one's mind.

Culture is also shaped by political power. Critics of ethnonationalism are fond of pointing out that many of today's nations, such as France, were constructed by tyrants. But this in no way implies that the French today should not resist the ambitions of tyrants who wish to replace them with blacks and Muslims. All human affairs are infected by contingency. None of our nations had to be. None of them are guaranteed to last forever. But that is simply all the more reason to fight against those who would replace us.

Love of One's Own

"This is who we are" is the final argument of identity politics. "Who we are" is a compound of kinship and culture. But identity is politically impotent unless a people is willing to assert itself, to take its own side in a fight. Thus the third pillar of white identity politics has to be that fighting spirit.

In his *Republic*, Plato divides the human soul into three parts: *reason*, which seeks truth; *desire*, which seeks the

---

[3] Here I am indebted to the anti-constructivist and conservative tradition in social theory that includes David Hume, Adam Smith, Edmund Burke, and Michael Polanyi.

necessities of life; and what one can call *fighting spirit* or *team spirit* (*thumos*), which is concerned with love of one's own and a willingness to fight for it.

Plato and Aristotle identified *thumos* as the specifically political part of the soul because *thumos* divides the world into us and them, ingroups and outgroups. In the twentieth century, the great German political philosopher Carl Schmitt argued that the very concept of the political[4] springs from the division between us and them, friend and enemy.

Desire and reason, by contrast, are implicitly anti-political because they unite us rather than divide us. Despite differences of language, history, and culture, we all desire the same basic necessities. Reason, moreover, seeks truth, which is objective and universal, meaning true for all of us.

When one talks about one's honor, family, or homeland, there is a different sense of ownership at work than when one talks about one's property. You own your property, but your property does not own you. The relationship of owner to property is one-way, not mutual or reciprocal. But our honor, family, or homeland are not external things, objects that we can pick up or discard casually. They are part of us. They define us. They are not alienable. We belong to them as much as they belong to us.

Genetic Similarity Theory explains the biological roots of loving one's own. Our selfish genes strive to perpetuate themselves into the future. But this does not lead to purely selfish individualism, because our genes are present in others, so it is advantageous to our genes for us to esteem, sympathize with, and in some cases sacrifice ourselves for others. But our genes are not equally distributed in all

---

[4] See Greg Johnson, "Reflections on Carl Schmitt's *The Concept of the Political*," *New Right vs. Old Right* (San Francisco: Counter-Currents, 2013).

other people. We share more genes with our kin than strangers, our countrymen than foreigners, and members of our race than members of other races. Therefore, it is natural for us to prefer those who are genetically "our own" over those who are genetically different.

Preferring people who are culturally "one's own" over foreigners is also quite understandable. Life is short, and social interactions are full of risks and uncertainty. It is easier to understand, trust, cooperate with, or just relax around people who share your language, customs, and values. Thus, other things being equal, it makes sense to prefer people who share one's culture.

In my speech "White Identity Politics: Inevitable, Necessary, Moral," I argued that there's nothing immoral about love of one's own. Here, I want to respond to some objections to love of one's own based on the ideas of *objective truth* and *objective merit*.

Love of one's own means prizing something based simply on its relationship to you. Love of one's own is inescapably "relative" to who one is. But shouldn't we prefer what is *objectively* true and good to what is merely one's own? The answer depends on context.

Love of one's own—specifically in the form of nationalism or other forms of partisanship—is irrelevant to determining the truth of objective historical facts or scientific theories. In Plato's terms, objective truths are the province of reason, not *thumos*. When *thumos* imperialistically intrudes into the realm of reason, objectivity is threatened.

It is inevitable that we invest our egos in our ideas, but the difference between a stubborn visionary and a vain fool is ultimately determined by objective facts.

It is also inevitable that national feeling influences one's approach to science and history. But nationalists become laughable when they promulgate fake histories: The Greeks stole their civilization from Africa, Irish is the original language of the Garden of Eden, a Brazilian invented the airplane, and the host of black invention myths. We also must reject extreme forms of relativism like the concepts of "Faustian mathematics" or "bourgeois physics."

But reason can also be imperialistic. The very idea of cosmopolitanism is a rationalistic construction. The ancient Greek natural philosophers believed that nature is uniform across space and time, but culture is not. Since the Greeks revered permanence and disdained change, the natural philosophers aspired to be citizens of unchanging nature rather than the mutable cities of men. Thus Diogenes of Sinope, the first Cynic, declared that the *cosmos* was his *polis*, that he was a citizen of the world (*kosmopolitês*). As I argue in "What's Wrong with Cosmopolitanism?," there are no actual citizens of the world, but the cosmopolitan idea is still used as an acid to weaken the thumotic ties that sustain real communities.[5]

There is no necessary contradiction between maintaining the objectivity of truth and natural preferences for one's own, including borders and immigration restrictions. First of all, if we limited immigration only to people possessing specialized knowledge and skills, that would reduce it to almost nothing. Second, because truths are objective and ideas are ideal, they can cross borders on their own. They don't need immigrants to carry them.

Even the transmission of skills from a master to an apprentice is not an argument for immigration, merely for travel. One can study abroad with a master, or masters can spend time abroad passing on their skills.

One of the most common arguments that spoiled and silly Westerners offer for diversity and immigration is their desire for a variety of ethnic restaurants. Of course

---

[5] Greg Johnson, "What's Wrong with Cosmopolitanism?," *In Defense of Prejudice*.

restaurants account for only a tiny fraction of immigration. But we can import recipes, skills, and ingredients without importing people.

What about objective merit? A strong nationalist preference for one's own people would naturally lead to little or no immigration. But shouldn't a country want the *best* doctors, scientists, engineers, and businessmen, no matter where they come from? Then why not open one's borders to the best?

First of all, this argument is not a case for *mass* immigration. If we are actually talking about the *best* in any field, that means we are talking about a very small number of people, not millions. Strict merit-based immigration would eliminate nearly all immigration today, the bulk of which is of low-skilled drones, welfare cases, and refugees.

Beyond that, accessing the *best* people is still not an argument for immigration. It is merely an argument for *travel*. No matter where he lives, the best brain surgeon in the world can only live in one country, maybe two, which means that the rest of the world has to come to him anyway. So why shouldn't he live in his native land? And if he travels to his patients, that is merely a business trip, not immigration.

Furthermore, if one isn't really talking about the best people in a profession, but people who are merely *good enough* for it, then surely every First World country already has sufficient numbers people who are good enough to be doctors, lawyers, scientists, engineers, and businessmen. We know this because many of those countries became "First World" without benefit of immigration, skilled or unskilled. Indeed, many of them saw massive emigration at the same time that they became modern powerhouses.

Beyond that, should First World countries really be importing highly skilled professionals from poor countries around the world? How do we expect these countries to improve themselves? Isn't there something absurd about First World countries importing doctors from the Third World while sending doctors on charity missions to the Third World?

But somehow many white people are convinced that immigration gives us access to the best of everything. I don't want to burst anybody's bubble, but how many of you have ever employed the services of the world's best *anything*? How many of you even have a snowball's chance of doing so? Is the average level of medical care in white countries really raised by doctors from the Middle East or South Asia? So is the phantom of meritocracy really worth the certainty of losing one's homeland to open borders? Especially when you consider that the only people in your homelands who are rich enough to access the best of everything are also rich enough to travel to get it.

The real reason our oligarchs promote "high-skilled" immigration is not the need for high skills but the desire to pay low wages. But if Google or Facebook really can't find enough qualified Americans, then they are welcome to send their capital to India rather than entice Indians to America.

But what about the best products? If the best cars and cameras are made in foreign lands, why shouldn't we import them? Of course this is an argument for trade, not immigration. One can let goods move freely but not people.

If the best cars and cameras are made overseas, one can frankly admit that. Facts are facts. But we can still have valid nationalist arguments against *buying* them—or making it easy to buy them. For instance, every country should aim at producing a significant amount of its own food and medicine, in case of global famines and pandemics. If this is so, then it is reasonable to protect key local industries from competition from foreign imports.

Moreover, governments raise money by taxes, and all

taxes have economic and social consequences, some good, some bad. Taxes on imported goods have positive consequences. They strengthen the nation by protecting local industries.

Finally, if we are really talking about the *best* cars or cameras, the small number of people who can afford the very best can also afford to pay import duties. Again, when people make arguments for free trade, they really aren't interested in the *best*—which only the rich can afford—but the *cheap,* which anyone can afford. Often these goods are so temptingly cheap because they are manufactured by people on starvation wages without worker safety and environmental regulations that are standard in decent societies.

Putting cheap foreign goods above the good of one's homeland is another form of imperialism, that of *desire,* working to corrode the thumotic sentiments that sustain a society. But cheap goods are very expensive when one calculates the full cost of importing them. You might enjoy buying cheap foreign shoes. But when local shoemakers go out of business, their employees won't be able to buy the goods you produce either. And since power follows money, as the rich get richer and the middle class grows poorer, society becomes less democratic and more elitist, which leads to injustice and instability.

As consumers, we pursue our private interests. As citizens, we need to look out for the common good. Left to their own devices, the masses will sell their birthrights for trinkets. Thus we need laws to ensure the common good comes first.

The idea of objective merit—objective truth, objective goodness—is highly appealing. It makes sense as rational agents pursuing truth and as rational consumers satisfying our needs. But it is deeply destructive to society when it insinuates itself into the realm of *thumos*.

We don't need any objective reasons at all to love our

own. Our children don't have to be the best for us to love them. Our homelands don't have to be the best for us to love them. Our race does not have to be the best for us to love it.

It is lonely at the top. In terms of any given excellence, only one child can be the best. Does that mean that no other children are lovable? By any given measure of excellence, only one country can truly be the best. Does that mean that no other homeland is loveable? In any given category, only one race is the best. Does that mean that members of all other races should despise themselves? Absolutely not.

National chauvinism and racial supremacism are foolish caricatures of love. We don't love our homelands because they are the best. We love them simply because they are ours. We don't love our race because it is the best but because it is ours. And unlike chauvinists and supremacists, we can love our own without denigrating others who love their own as well. Indeed, we can understand why they do so, and neither party need feel threatened by the other.

Does one have to *do anything*—aside from being part of someone's family, nation, or race—to be on the receiving end of love of one's own? Since the ownness we are speaking about is mutual and reciprocal—if our family, homeland, and race belong to us, and we belong to them—then the love we receive should also be reciprocated. But when we are born, we can't really *pay back* the care we receive. We can only *pay it forward*, to the next generation. Love of our own is a birthright that we claim of others and an inherited obligation that the next generation claims of us.

None of this is visible to the modern liberal. Modern man sees himself as a rational producer-consumer. From that point of view, there are no nations. Reason and desire embrace the whole cosmos. They have no homelands.

Modernity claims that all men are equal, meaning that natural preferences and human borders are illegitimate.

In practice, this means that all men are interchangeable, which means that you are replaceable with foreigners. The Great Replacement is merely the political expression of a world-destroying blindness, what Heidegger called the essence of technology: the decision to see the world—and ourselves—as merely a stockpile of interchangeable resources.

The globalists have not refuted nationalism. They are simply blind to us and our concerns. When confronted with human differences, they airily declare that they do not matter. Identitarians beg to differ. In fact, we insist on it. In fact, we'll fight to preserve our differences.

The answer to the Great Replacement is simply to say "No." We will not jump into the melting pot. We veto the globalist dream.

Let's call it the Great Refusal. Alfred North Whitehead borrowed this phrase from Dante and gave it a new meaning: the imagination's refusal to be confined by facts. It is the power of consciousness to negate the given. Herbert Marcuse adopted the phrase to refer to the rejection of a dehumanizing consumer society for the liberating power of art.

For Identitarians, the Great Refusal is the thumotic reassertion of difference in the face of the Great Replacement. We are not equal. We are not interchangeable. This is who we are, and so we will remain. You will not replace us.

Counter-Currents, October 7, 8, & 26, 2020

THE VERY IDEA OF WHITE PRIVILEGE*

I want to thank Fróði Midjord and the rest of the Scandza team for making this event possible, as well as all of you for coming out to hear me. I am honored today to be speaking alongside these distinguished doctors of the human sciences.

My Ph.D., however, is in philosophy. Philosophers don't do scientific research. Instead, we stand back and try to talk about the big picture, including the meaning of scientific discoveries for politics and morals. My topic today is "The Very Idea of White Privilege."

A *privilege* is an advantage that you enjoy and others don't. Privilege is inherently unequal. Special privileges are the opposite of equal rights. *White privilege* means advantages enjoyed by whites just in virtue of their race—rights not enjoyed by non-whites. White privilege is a form of *hereditary* privilege. Whites do nothing to earn or merit white privilege over and above simply being born. White privilege thus refers to a whole range of unequal and unearned—and thus unjust—advantages enjoyed by whites and denied to non-whites in the societies that whites created. White privilege is just another word for white "racism."

The concept of white privilege has exploded in American public discourse in the last five years, coinciding with the so-called "great awokening," the wave of Left-wing

---

* This lecture was written for the Scandza Forum's conference on Human Bio-Diversity in Oslo, Norway, on November 2, 2019, but it was not delivered by order of the Norwegian secret police. See Greg Johnson, "Anarcho-Tyranny in Oslo," *Counter-Currents*, November 6, 2019.

hysteria and gaslighting set off by the Trayvon Martin and Michael Brown hoaxes, namely the claims that two blacks who were killed while committing crimes were actually the real victims, innocent victims of white racism.

The concept of white privilege has provoked a great deal of eye-rolling and healthy anger from whites. This manifestation of white toughness has, absurdly, been termed "white fragility," which is a clear sign that the Left is not just out of touch with reality but simply thinks that it can be conjured up or banished with magic words.

Whites reject the idea of white privilege for various reasons.

- Some think that racism is a terrible thing, but they don't think that they or their societies are guilty of it.
- The vast majority of white people work very hard and never had anything given to them, so they resent the idea that they benefit from unearned privileges.
- Others think there is nothing wrong with racial inequality and believe that white privilege is just another politically correct moral swindle in which non-whites seek unearned advantages by accusing good-hearted whites of spurious offenses for which they can buy forgiveness.

But as much as I applaud this pushback against white privilege, the concept is not entirely meaningless. For instance, within the lifetimes of some people present today, whites enjoyed legal privileges denied to non-whites in Apartheid South Africa and the American South.

But there is not a white society in the world today in which whites enjoy such legal privileges over non-whites. Even the idea of nationality through descent is being chipped away as a form of privilege. Indeed, in South Africa and the United States, non-whites now enjoy privileges over whites, both legally and through massive private discrimination.

Yet, even with decades of official and unofficial non-white privilege behind us, certain non-white groups are more likely than whites to be uneducated, poor, and in trouble with the law—to name just three important factors in overall social well-being.

The official explanation for these lingering inequalities is "racism," that is to say: white malevolence, as well as "systemic" forms of inequality. According to this theory, since all people want to thrive in white societies and have equal inherent potential to do so, the fact that some groups conspicuously do not thrive needs to be explained.

Since white people are the architects of these societies, we are obviously the ones to blame. Thus white people must be hectored and browbeaten and reeducated. We must be punished by affirmative action and reparations. And we must endure having our societies torn apart and rebuilt over and over again, until racial equality is attained. Because nothing stands in the way of racial equality except white institutions and ways of life, white ignorance and ill-will, white guilt and white privilege—or so they say.

But it is increasingly difficult to believe this viewpoint because white legal privileges have been overturned. White privilege has not, moreover, been replaced by a classical liberal meritocracy, in which all people are subject to the same rules and judged on individual merit, but by a system of non-white privilege. But even with the system rigged in their favor, some non-white groups conspicuously lag behind whites in a vast number of indexes of social well-being.[1]

---

[1] An excellent summation of these differences is Richard Lynn's *The Global Bell Curve: Race, IQ, and Inequality Worldwide*

Even though anti-racist activists and non-whites find it increasingly difficult to point to any specific cause of persistent inequality, they *just know* that it is *somehow* white people's fault. This is why the Left has resorted to increasingly "occult"—i.e. hidden and mysterious—explanations for persistent racial inequality.

Since fewer and fewer whites are *consciously* racist, the problem must be *unconscious* racism *somehow* keeping certain groups down. Unconscious racism is a real phenomenon, but how far does it explain persistent inequality?[2]

Since fewer and fewer whites hold negative racial stereotypes about other groups, yet non-whites still display stereotypical behavior, non-whites must be sabotaging themselves because of the "threat"—the mere specter—of negative stereotypes existing in their own minds. And this is still white people's fault, *somehow*.

Since explicit, legal racism has been dismantled and even reversed, the legacy of past racism must still exert a subtle influence that is powerful enough to cancel out the effects of much more recent systems of non-white privilege, *somehow*.

The classic statement on white privilege is Peggy McIntosh's 1989 essay, "White Privilege: Unpacking the Invisible Knapsack," where she writes:

> I have come to see white privilege as an invisible package of unearned assets that I can count on cashing in each day, but about which I was "meant" to remain oblivious. White privilege is like an invisible weightless knapsack of special provisions, maps,

---

(Augusta, Ga.: Washington Summit Publishers, 2008).

[2] On unconscious racism, see Kevin MacDonald's "Psychology and White Ethnocentrism," *The Occidental Quarterly*, vol. 6, no. 4 (2006).

> passports, codebooks, visas, clothes, tools, and blank checks.[3]

McIntosh offers fifty examples of white privilege. McIntosh's backpack is more of a grab bag, ranging from discrimination in housing and law enforcement to the color of band-aids. McIntosh's examples make it very clear that when she speaks of non-white Americans she is thinking specifically of black Americans.

Most of McIntosh's white privileges fall into two broad categories: (1) aspects of having a homeland, and (2) not being black. Aspects of having a homeland include:

> 1. I can if I wish arrange to be in the company of people of my race most of the time.
>
> 2. I can avoid spending time with people whom I was trained to mistrust and who have learned to mistrust my kind or me.
>
> 6. I can turn on the television or open to the front page of the paper and see people of my race widely represented.
>
> 7. When I am told about our national heritage or about "civilization," I am shown that people of my color made it what it is.
>
> 8. I can be sure that my children will be given curricular materials that testify to the existence of their race.
>
> 12. I can go into a music shop and count on finding

[3] Peggy McIntosh, "White Privilege: Unpacking the Invisible Knapsack," *Peace & Freedom Magazine* (July/August 1989), pp. 10–12.

the music of my race represented, into a supermarket and find the staple foods which fit with my cultural traditions, into a hairdresser's shop and find someone who can cut my hair.

14. I can arrange to protect my children most of the time from people who might not like them.

15. I do not have to educate my children to be aware of systemic racism for their own daily physical protection.

16. I can be pretty sure that my children's teachers and employers will tolerate them if they fit school and workplace norms; my chief worries about them do not concern others' attitudes toward their race.

23. I can criticize our government and talk about how much I fear its policies and behavior without being seen as a cultural outsider.

24. I can be pretty sure that if I ask to talk to the "person in charge," I will be facing a person of my race.

26. I can easily buy posters, post-cards, picture books, greeting cards, dolls, toys, and children's magazines featuring people of my race.

27. I can go home from most meetings of organizations I belong to feeling somewhat tied in, rather than isolated, out-of-place, outnumbered, unheard, held at a distance, or feared.

32. My culture gives me little fear about ignoring the perspectives and powers of people of other races.

46. I can choose blemish cover or bandages in "flesh" color and have them more or less match my skin.

All of these "privileges" are simply aspects of having a homogeneous homeland, of belonging to a community of people with whom you share a common biological and cultural heritage. In white societies, one can call this "white privilege." But in Asian societies, one would call it "Asian privilege" and in African societies, "African privilege." Furthermore, it is too crude to speak about privilege simply in terms of broad racial categories. Instead, we should speak about Norwegian privilege in Norway, Japanese privilege in Japan, Swazi privilege in Swaziland, and the like. It would also be nice to live in a world in which stateless peoples, like Palestinians and Kurds, have similar privileges.

McIntosh describes privilege as "invisible" and "weightless." We are "oblivious" of privilege. The unconscious aspect of privilege is also an aspect of having a homeland. A homeland is not just a realm in space. It is also a realm of meaning. To be truly at home, one must fully internalize and master these codes of meaning—language and manners being the most important—so one does not have to consciously reflect on them. Then one can simply relax and *live* rather than be self-conscious.

A foreign land is not just a place with unfamiliar people and things. The conventions are unfamiliar as well, thus one is constantly forced to reflect upon things that are taken for granted by the natives. Is this the right word? Is this the right greeting? How do I call 911?

It is fun to visit foreign lands, but it can be alienating, stressful, and psychologically exhausting to actually live in one, and this is the everyday experience of minorities and stateless peoples in other people's homelands. The cure to this problem is to give every people a land of their own where they can feel at home rather than constantly alienated.

Many of McIntosh's alleged privileges of being white are more accurately described as *the absence of the disadvantages of being black*. These include:

> 3. If I should need to move, I can be pretty sure of renting or purchasing housing in an area which I can afford and in which I would want to live.
>
> 4. I can be pretty sure that my neighbors in such a location will be neutral or pleasant to me.
>
> 5. I can go shopping alone most of the time, pretty well assured that I will not be followed or harassed.
>
> 13. Whether I use checks, credit cards, or cash, I can count on my skin color not to work against the appearance of financial reliability.
>
> 18. I can swear, or dress in secondhand clothes, or not answer letters, without having people attribute these choices to the bad morals, the poverty, or the illiteracy of my race.
>
> 19. I can speak in public to a powerful male group without putting my race on trial.
>
> 25. If a traffic cop pulls me over or if the IRS audits my tax return, I can be sure I haven't been singled out because of my race.
>
> 35. I can take a job with an affirmative action employer without having my co-workers on the job suspect that I got it because of my race.
>
> 36. If my day, week, or year is going badly, I need

not ask of each negative episode or situation whether it had racial overtones.

38. I can think over many options, social, political, imaginative, or professional, without asking whether a person of my race would be accepted or allowed to do what I want to do.

39. I can be late to a meeting without having the lateness reflect on my race.

40. I can choose public accommodation without fearing that people of my race cannot get in or will be mistreated in the places I have chosen.

41. I can be sure that if I need legal or medical help, my race will not work against me.

43. If I have low credibility as a leader I can be sure that my race is not the problem.

McIntosh describes black disadvantages as white privileges because she wishes to absolve blacks for these problems and blame whites. Unfortunately, many anti-black stereotypes—for instance, black criminality and financial irresponsibility—are not just dreamed up by evil-minded white people. They are based in experience.

Of course most blacks are not criminals and spendthrifts, but enough of them are that it is rational for whites to be vigilant around blacks they do not know, a burden of suspicion that falls equally upon the problem minority and the blameless majority.

It really is an injustice. But it is also rational. Thus whites should not feel guilty about it. Such rational distrust is an inevitable product of diversity, and it will only increase as our societies become more multicultural. The

Left's only response to the rational distrust generated by diversity is to morally shame whites into dropping their guard, making them more vulnerable to predators and parasites.

One of the central contentions of the Black Lives Matter movement is that blacks are arrested for crimes at a greater rate than whites simply because of white racism. But objective data show that *blacks are arrested for crimes at pretty much the same rate that they commit them.*[4] Thus, if Black Lives Matter wishes to lower the black arrest rate, they should work to lower the black crime rate.

But there is not a single politician in America who has the courage to simply tell blacks to commit fewer crimes. Instead, police departments are being intimidated into giving blacks license to break the law with impunity. Police are also more likely to use violence with white suspects than blacks in comparable situations. This is objectively a system of black privilege.[5]

Blacks feel oppressed in white societies by negative white stereotypes. But the most momentous of these stereotypes are based in experience. Thus it is rational to use them as guides in dealing with black strangers. Because of this, no amount of reeducation is going to banish them.[6]

As long as multiracial societies persist, whites will continue to resent blacks for not living up to white standards,

---

[4] See for instance, Edwin S. Rubenstein's *The Color of Crime: Race, Crime, and Justice in America* (Oakton, Vir.: New Century Foundation, 2016).

[5] On Black Lives Matter and the collapse of policing blacks, see Heather MacDonald's many studies on "the Ferguson effect." On the over-policing of whites in America, including increased chances of death by cop, see Richard Houck's "Law Enforcement and the Hostile Elite," *Counter-Currents*, June 20, 2018.

[6] For a more detailed discussion of the rationality of experience-based prejudices, see my essay "In Defense of Prejudice," in *In Defense of Prejudice* and *It's Okay to Be White.*

and blacks will continue to resent whites for imposing alien standards. The ethnonationalist solution to such irreconcilable differences is racial divorce: the creation of homogeneous sovereign homelands, to the extent that this is possible, for all distinct peoples who wish to exercise this right.

The main reason to reject the claim that America is a white supremacist society is the fact that some non-white groups—chiefly East Asians and certain communities of South Asians—do better than whites in key indicators of success, such as educational attainment, income, and law abidingness, and they did so before anti-white discrimination and non-white tokenism became rampant. If American whites were intent on creating systematic white privilege and supremacy, we failed miserably. Therefore, white racism is not a sufficient explanation for differing racial outcomes in America.

We have an alternative hypothesis based on the science of Human Biological Diversity. The differing levels of education, income, and law-abidingness—to name just three factors—among racial groups in America are precisely what we would predict given measurable differences of IQ and sociopathic personality traits between the races. For a survey of the effect of IQ on a wide range of social outcomes, see Richard Lynn's *The Global Bell Curve*. On racial differences in personality traits beyond just IQ, including psychopathy, see Michael Levin's *Why Race Matters*.[7]

This does not mean that the American system is "fair" in the sense of being a color-blind meritocracy. We are perfectly willing to admit that some forms of discrimination favor whites—if it is also acknowledged that significant non-white privileges exist. But I believe that Human

[7] Michael Levin's *Why Race Matters* (Oakton, Vir.: New Century Books, 2016).

Biological Diversity is so powerful a determinant of social outcomes that it can basically overpower both white and anti-white privileges, allowing us to act *as if* these forces do not exist, even though we know that they do. In a similar way, although we know that other measurable psychological traits matter to social outcomes, IQ differences alone are so powerful at predicting social outcomes that we can act *as if* other factors do not exist. (This was brought home to me by Lynn's *The Global Bell Curve.*)

Different races really are different. That means that when different races live in the same social system, subject to the same laws, institutions, and incentives, some will inevitably flourish better than others. There will never be a social system that is equally conducive to the flourishing of all races and cultures. Such inequalities will persist even if we institute remedial forms of discrimination in favor of groups who lag behind. The science of Human Biological Diversity also explains why some non-white groups excel in white societies, even though they too have trouble finding flesh-colored band-aids.

Many of us would prefer not to mention biological racial differences at all, for fear of hurting the feelings of disadvantaged groups. But we have to talk about such differences, because the present system blames whites for the failure of some non-whites to flourish in white societies. As long as whites are charged with evil intentions to keep some races down, and as long as white institutions and ways of life are targeted for demolition and reconstruction by egalitarian social engineers, we must press the alternative hypothesis of biologically based inequality.

So if the different races are biologically unequal, what does this imply for social policy? Today's conservatives and libertarians think they can retain multiculturalism by establishing a true "color-blind" meritocracy. While I am all for meritocracy, it is simply naïve to believe that groups that will naturally gravitate toward the bottom of such a system—the "losers"—will be satisfied with their lot, even if they arrived there by entirely "fair" procedures, and even if they enjoy higher material standards of living than they could in non-white homelands.

Classical liberalism is simply blind to non-material motivations like honor and pride. Many non-whites would rather rule in hell (their own homelands) than serve in heaven (classical liberal meritocracies). Ethnonationalists, however, understand completely.

Every human being deserves a home, where he can be himself free of the interference of others. But we should feel at home outside our front doors as well. We should be able to live among people who share our language and values, our history and destiny, the whole litany of "white privileges." We don't just need homes. We need homelands. Not alienating, bewildering, multicultural bazaars filled with people who do not share our language and values. A country's Gross Domestic Product does not matter if nobody feels at home.

If races really are different, that means they will create different social systems. These systems will express their natures. They will feel as comfortable to them as well-fitting shoes. But this means that other races will not feel comfortable, even if they are treated with utmost courtesy and fairness—even if they are given advantages over the natives. The solution is not to further change our societies, to further abandon our norms and ways of life to accommodate outsiders. That simply doesn't work. Multiculturalism does not create societies where everyone feels at home. It creates societies where no one feels at home.

There is no moral imperative to destroy our homelands to accommodate strangers. There would be no such imperative even if it were possible. And there is certainly no imperative to destroy real homelands in pursuit of the impossible dream of a society in which all peoples feel equally at home.

But there is one place where all the peoples of the world can feel at home. It is called the planet Earth. This planet is big enough for all races and nations to have places they can call their own. This is the ethnonationalist version of utopia. Privilege is inherently unequal. But everyone can be privileged in his own homeland. Norwegians can be privileged in Norway. Somalis can be privileged in Somalia. Kurds can be privileged in Kurdistan. As long as every people has a place to call home, there is nothing unfair about this situation.

Peggy McIntosh describes white privilege as a package of "unearned assets." That is meant as a criticism. But we must be careful here. Only a bourgeois individualist equates the unearned with the unjust. There are some cases where we have a right to unearned assets. For instance, if a gift truly is a gift, and not simply a disguised form of exchange, then it is an unearned asset to which we have a right. A gift created by past generations and handed on to future generations cannot be a disguised exchange, for there is no way to pay our ancestors back for our genetic and cultural heritage. We can only pay it forward, to future generations. A homeland is an unearned asset, a privilege, and you have every right to defend it zealously.

Norway is not something that all people can enjoy. It is something for yourselves and your posterity. It was created by your ancestors, carved out of a remarkably harsh environment through will and ingenuity. It was passed on to you, for safekeeping and improvement. And I hope you will pass it along to future generations once strangers like me have left your shores.

Counter-Currents, November 8, 2019

In Defense of Populism*

The Specter of Populism

The populist uprisings of 2016—Brexit and the election of Donald Trump—aren't epochal events like the revolutions of 1789 and 1848. Not yet anyway. But you wouldn't know that judging from the panic that swept through Western political elites.

Bernard-Henri Lévy denounced Brexit as the "victory of the most rancid form of sovereignty and the most idiotic form of nationalism"; Jacques Attali decried the "dictatorship of populism"; Alain Minc lamented the victory "of ill-educated people over the well-educated"; and Daniel Cohn-Bendit simply exclaimed, "I'm sick of the people!"[1]

European Commission president Jean-Claude Juncker warned against "galloping populism"; the Tony Blair Institute for Global Change declared that populists "pose a real threat to democracy itself"; and Pope Francis, who knows something about good and evil, admonished the world that, "Populism is evil and ends badly."[2]

It is quite commonplace for journalists and politicians to denigrate populist voters as a "rabble" or a "mob" motivated by "ignorance," "fear," and "hatred," including "racism" and "xenophobia." They also characterize populist politicians as "demagogues" who "pander" to the worst

---

* This lecture was written for the Scandza Forum in Copenhagen, Denmark on October 12, 2019, but it was not delivered because Antifa besieged the venue and prevented me from entering.

[1] Quoted in Alain de Benoist, "What Is Populism?" in *Democracy and Populism: The* Telos *Essays*, ed. Russell A. Berman and Timothy W. Luke (Candor, N.Y.: Telos Press, 2018), p. 335.

[2] Quoted in Benjamin Moffitt, *Populism* (London: Polity, 2020), p. 2.

instincts of the mob—unlike the edifying statesmen of the center-Left and center-Right.

Populism seeks to rescue popular government from corrupt elites. It is no surprise that the elites strike back. What is surprising, though, are their frank expressions of fear and hatred of the people, which can only strengthen populist convictions. Such self-defeating behavior is ultimately encouraging. Elites this arrogant and impulsive have little future.

I wish to defend populism from two elite criticisms.

First, populism is commonly accused of being "anti-democratic." Yascha Mounk frames populism as "the people vs. democracy."[3] I argue that populism is not anti-democratic, but it is anti-liberal.

Second, many critics of populism accuse it of being a form of white identity politics, and many critics of white identity politics accuse it of being populist. I argue that populism and white identity politics are distinct but sometimes overlapping phenomena. Populism and white identity politics do, however, *complement* one another, so that the strongest form of white identity politics is populist, and the strongest form of populism is identitarian.

First, though, we need to clarify what populism really is.

POLITICAL IDEOLOGY OR POLITICAL STYLE?

One of the more superficial claims about populism is that it is not a political ideology but simply a "political style." An ideology is a set of principles. A political style is a way of embodying and communicating political principles. The idea that populism is merely a political style is based on the observation that there are populisms of the

---

[3] Yascha Mounk, *The People vs. Democracy: Why Our Freedom is in Danger and How to Save It* (Cambridge: Harvard University Press, 2018).

Left and the Right, so how could it be a unified ideology? Of course, there are also liberalisms of the Left and Right, but this does not imply that liberalism is merely a style of politics rather than a political ideology.

PRINCIPLES OF POPULISM

What is the ideology of populism? What are its basic principles? Just as Right and Left liberalism appeal to common political principles, Right and Left populists also have the same basic political ideas:

- All populists appeal to the principle of popular sovereignty. *Sovereignty* means that a people is independent of other peoples. A sovereign nation is master of its own internal affairs. It can pursue its own ends, as opposed to being subordinated to the ends of others, such as a foreign people or a monarch. The sovereignty of the people is the idea that legitimate government is "of the people, by the people, for the people," meaning that (1) the people must somehow participate in government, i.e., that they govern themselves, and (2) the state acts in the interest of the people as a whole, i.e., for the common good.
- All populists politically mobilize on the premise that popular government has been betrayed by a tiny minority of political insiders, who have arrogated the people's right to self-government and who govern for their own factional interests, or foreign interests, but not in the interest of the people as a whole. Populists declare that the political system is in crisis.
- All populists hold that the sovereignty of the people must be restored (1) by ensuring greater popular participation in politics and (2) by re-

> placing traitorous elites with loyal servants of the people. Populists thus frame themselves as redeeming popular sovereignty from a crisis.

Two Senses of "the People"

When populists say the people are sovereign, they mean *the people as a whole*. When populists oppose "the people" to "the elites," they are contrasting *the vast majority*, who are political outsiders, to the elites, who are political insiders. The goal of populism, however, is to restore the unity of the sovereign people by eliminating the conflicts of interest between the elites and the people.

Ethnic & Civic Peoplehood

There are two basic ways of defining a people: *ethnic* and *civic*. An ethnic group is unified by blood, culture, and history. An ethnic group is an extended family with a common language and history. Ethnic groups always emerge in a particular place but do not necessarily remain there.

A civic conception of peoplehood is a construct that seeks to impose unity on a society composed of different ethnic groups, lacking a common descent, culture, and history. For instance, civic nationalists claim that a person can become British, American, or Danish simply by government *fiat*, i.e., by being given *legal* citizenship.

Ethnic nationalism draws strength from unity and homogeneity. Ethnically defined groups grow primarily through reproduction, although they have always recognized that some foreigners can be "naturalized"—i.e., "assimilated" into the body politic—although rarely and with much effort.

Civic nationalism lacks the strength of unity but aims to mitigate that weakness by constructing and imposing a civic ideology. Civic nationalists also hope to offset diversity with strength in numbers, since in principle the whole world can have identity papers issued by a central state.

A civic people is a pure social construct imposed on a set of particular human beings that need not have anything more in common than walking on two legs and having citizenship papers. Civic conceptions of peoplehood thus go hand in hand with the radical nominalist position that only individuals, not collectives, exist in the real world. Groups are mere "social constructs."

An ethnic people is much more than a social construct. First of all, kinship groups are real biological collectives. Beyond that, although ethnic groups are distinguished from other biologically similar groups by differences of language, culture, and history, there is a distinction between evolved social practices like language and culture and mere legislative fiats and other social constructs.

Ethnic peoples exist even without their own states. There are many stateless peoples in the world. But civic peoples do not exist without a state. Civic polities are constructs of the elites that control states.

Populism & Elitism

Populism is contrasted with elitism. But populists are not against elites as such. Populists oppose elites for two main reasons: when they are not *part* of the people and when they *exploit* the people. Populists approve of elites that are organically part of the people and function as servants of the people as a whole.

Populists recognize that people differ in terms of intelligence, virtue, and skills. Populists want to have the best qualified people in important offices. But they want to ensure that elites work for the common good of the polity, not for their own factional interests (or foreign interests). To ensure this, populists wish to empower the people to check the power of elites, as well as to create new elites that are organically connected to the people and who put the common good above their private interests.

POPULISM & CLASSICAL REPUBLICANISM

When political scientists and commentators discuss the history of populism, most begin with nineteenth-century agrarian movements like the Narodniki in Russia and the People's Party in the United States. But nineteenth-century populism looked back to the republics of the ancient world, specifically the "mixed regime" of Rome.

Aristotle's *Politics* is the most influential theory of the mixed regime.[4] Aristotle observed that a society can be ruled by one man, a few men, or many men. But a society can never be ruled by *all* men, since every society inevitably includes people who are incapable of participating in government due to lack of ability, for instance the very young, the crazy, and the senile.

Aristotle also observed that the one, few, or many could govern for their *factional* interests or for the *common good*. When one man governs for the common good, we have *monarchy*. When he governs for his private interests, we have *tyranny*. When the few govern for the common good, we have *aristocracy*. When the few govern for their private interests, we have *oligarchy*. When the many govern for the common good, we have *polity*. When the many govern for their factional interests, we have *democracy*.

It is interesting that for Aristotle, democracy is bad *by definition* and that he had to invent a new word, "polity," for the good kind of popular rule that was, presumably, so rare that nobody had yet coined a term for it.

Aristotle recognized that government by one man or few men is always government by the rich, regardless of whether wealth is used to purchase political power or

[4] See Greg Johnson, "Introduction to Aristotle's *Politics*," *From Plato to Postmodernism* (San Francisco: Counter-Currents, 2019).

whether political power is used to secure wealth. Thus popular government always empowers those who lack wealth. The extremely poor, however, tend to be alienated, servile, and greedy. But self-employed, middle-class citizens have a stake in the future, long time-horizons, and sufficient leisure to participate in politics. Thus popular government tends to be stable when it empowers the middle class and chaotic when it empowers the poorest elements.

Finally, Aristotle recognized that a regime that mixes together rule by the one, the few, and the many is more likely to achieve the common good, not simply because each group is public-spirited, but also because they are all jealous to protect their private interests from being despoiled by the rest. Aristotle was thus the first theorist of the "mixed regime." But he was simply observing the functioning of actually existing mixed regimes like Sparta.

One can generate modern populism quite easily from Aristotle's premises. Aristotle's idea of the common good is the basis of the idea of *popular sovereignty*, which means, first and foremost, that *legitimate government must look out for the common good of the people*.

Beyond that, Aristotle argued that the best way to ensure legitimate government is to empower the many—specifically the middle class—to participate in government. The default position of every society is to be governed by the one or the few. When the elites govern selfishly and oppress the people, the people naturally wish to rectify this by demanding participation in government. They can, of course, use their power simply to satisfy their factional interests, which is why democracy has always been feared. But if popular rule is unjust, it is also unstable. Thus to be stable and salutary, popular rule must aim at the common good of society.

The great theorist of popular sovereignty is Jean-Jacques Rousseau. In his *On the Social Contract*, Rousseau claims that the General Will is the fount of sovereignty and legitimacy. What is the General Will? The General Will wills the common good. The common good is not a convention or construct of the General Will but rather an objective fact that must be discovered and then realized through political action.

Rousseau distinguishes the General Will from the Will of All. The General Will is what we *ought* to will. The Will of All is what we *happen* to will. The Will of All can be wrong, however. Thus we cannot determine the General Will simply by polling the people.

Rousseau even holds out the possibility that an elite, or a dictator, can know the General Will better than the populace at large.[5] But no matter how the General Will is determined—and no matter who controls the levers of power—political legitimacy arises from the common good of the people.

Populism & Representation

Populism is often associated with "direct" as opposed to "representative" democracy. Populists tend to favor referendums and plebiscites, in which the electorate as a whole decides on important issues, as opposed to allowing them to be decided by representatives in parliament. In truth, though, there is no such thing as direct democracy in which the whole of the people acts. Even in plebiscites, some people always represent the interests of others. Thus democracy always requires some degree of representation.

One can only vote in the present. But a people is not just its present members. It also consists of its past members and its future members. Our ancestors matter to us. They created a society and passed it on to us. They estab-

---

[5] See Greg Johnson, "Forced to Be Free: The Case for Paternalism," *Confessions of a Reluctant Hater*, 2nd ed. (San Francisco: Counter-Currents, 2016).

lished standards by which we measure ourselves. And just as our ancestors lived not just for themselves, but for their posterity, people today make decisions that affect future generations. Thus in every democratic decision, the living must represent the interests of the dead and the not yet born.

Moreover, within the present generation, some are too young to participate in politics. Others are unable due to disability. The basic principle for excluding living people from the electorate is that they would lower the quality of political decision-making. However, they are still part of the people and have legitimate interests. Thus the electorate must represent their interests as well.

Beyond that, there are distinctions among competent adults that may lead to further constriction of the electorate, again to raise the quality of political decision-making. For instance, people have argued that the franchise should be restricted to men (because they are the natural guardians of society or because they are more rational than women), or to people with property (because they have more to lose), or to people with children (because they have a greater stake in the future), or to military veterans (because they have proven themselves willing to die, if necessary, for the common good). But again, all of those who are excluded from the franchise are still part of the people, with interests that must be respected. So they must be represented by the electorate.

Thus even in a plebiscite, the people as a whole is represented by only a part, the electorate. Beyond that, unless voting is mandatory, not every member of the electorate will choose to vote. So those who do not vote are represented by those who do.

Thus far, this thought experiment has not even gotten to the question of *representative* democracy, which takes the process one step further. An elected representative may stand for hundreds of thousands or millions of voters.

And those voters in turn stand for eligible non-voters, as well as those who are not eligible to vote, and beyond that, those who are not present to vote because they are dead or not yet born. The not-yet-born is an indefinite number that we hope is infinite, meaning that our people never dies. It seems miraculous that such a multitude could ever be represented by a relative handful of representatives (in the US, 535 Representatives and Senators for more than 300 million living people and untold billions of the dead and yet-to-be born). Bear in mind, also, that practically every modern politician will eagerly claim to be really thinking about the good of the entire human race.

But we have not yet scaled the highest peak, for people quite spontaneously think of the president, prime minister, or monarch—a single individual—as representing the interests of the entire body politic. Even if that is not their constitutional role, there are circumstances—such as emergencies—in which such leaders are expected to intuit the common good and act accordingly.

Thus it is not surprising that cynics wish to claim that the very ideas of a sovereign people, a common good, and the ability to represent them in politics are simply myths and mumbo-jumbo. Wouldn't it be better to replace such myths with concrete realities, like selfish individuals and value-neutral institutions that let them peacefully pursue their own private goods?

But the sovereign individual and the "invisible hand" are actually more problematic than the sovereign people and its avatars. From direct democracy in small towns to the popular uprisings that brought down communism, we have actual examples of sovereign peoples manifesting themselves and exercising power. We have actual examples of leaders representing a sovereign people, divining the common good, and acting to secure it.

There is no question *that* sovereign peoples actually exercise power for their common goods. But *how* it happens seems like magic. This explains why popular sovereignty is always breaking down. Which in turn explains why populist movements keep arising to return power to the people.

POPULISM & DEMOCRACY

Now we can understand why populism is not anti-democratic. Populism is simply another word for democracy, understood as popular sovereignty plus political empowerment of the many. Current elites claim that populism threatens "democracy" because they are advocates of specifically *liberal* democracy.

Liberal democrats claim to protect the rights of the individual and of minorities from unrestrained majoritarianism. Liberal democrats also defend "pluralism." Finally, liberal democrats insist that the majority is simply not competent to participate directly in government, thus they must be content to elect representatives from an established political class and political parties. These representatives, moreover, give great latitude to unelected technocrats in the permanent bureaucracy.

Liberal democracy is, in short, anti-majoritarian and elitist. Populists recognize that such regimes *can* work for the public good, as long as the ruling elites are part of the people and see themselves as its servants. But without the oversight and empowerment of the people, there is nothing to prevent liberal democracy from mutating into the rule of corrupt elites for their private interests and for foreign interests. This is why populism is on the rise: to root out corruption and restore popular sovereignty and the common good.

Populists need not reject liberal protections for individuals and minorities, ethnic or political. They need not reject "pluralism" when it is understood as freedom of opinion and multiparty democracy. Populists don't even reject elites, political representation, and technocratic competence. Populists can value all of these things. But they value the common good of the people even more, and they recognize that liberal values don't *necessarily* serve the common good. When they don't, they need to be brought into line. Liberals, however, tend to put their ideology above the common good, leading to the corruption of popular government. Ideological liberalism is a disease of democracy. Populism is the cure.

Populism & White Identity Politics

What is the connection between populism and white identity politics? I am both a populist and an advocate of white identity politics. But there are advocates of white identity politics who are anti-populist (for instance, those who are influenced by Traditionalism and monarchism), and there are non-white populists around the world (for instance, Rodrigo Duterte in the Philippines and Thaksin Shinawatra in Thailand).

However, even if there is no *necessary* connection between populism and white identity politics, I wish to argue that the two movements should work together in every white country. White identitarians will be strengthened by populism, and populism will be strengthened by appeals to white identity.

Why should white identitarians align ourselves with populism? Roger Eatwell and Matthew Goodwin argue in *National Populism: The Revolt Against Liberal Democracy* that the rise of national populism is motivated by what they call "the Four Ds." The first is Distrust, namely the breakdown of public trust in government. The second is Destruction, specifically the destruction of *identity*, the destruction of the *ethnic composition* of their homelands due to immigration and multiculturalism. The third trend is Deprivation, referring to the collapse of First-World living standards, especially middle-class and working-class living standards, due to globalization. The final trend is Dealignment, meaning the abandonment of the center-Left, center-Right duopolies common in post-Second World War democracies.

The Destruction of identity due to immigration and multiculturalism is a central issue for white identitarians. The Deprivation caused by globalization is also one of our central issues. The only way to fix these problems is to adopt white identitarian policies, namely to put the interests and identity of indigenous whites first. If that principle is enshrined, everything we want follows of course. It is just a matter of time and will.

As for Distrust and Dealignment, these can go for or against us, but we can certainly *relate* to them, and we can *contribute* to and *shape* them as well.

Eatwell and Goodwin argue that the "Four Ds" have deep roots and will be affecting politics for decades to come. National populism is the wave of the future, and we should ride it to political power.

Why do populists need to appeal to white identity? It all comes down to what counts as the people. Is the people at its core an ethnic group, or is it defined in purely civic terms? Populists of the Right appeal explicitly or implicitly to identitarian issues. Populists of the Left prefer to define the people in civic or class terms and focus on economic issues. Since, as Eatwell and Goodwin argue, *both* identitarian and economic issues are driving the rise of populism, populists of the Right will have a broader appeal because they appeal to both identity and economic issues.

The great task of white identitarians today is to destroy the legitimacy of civic nationalism and push the populism of the Right toward explicit white identitarianism.

Justifying Popular Sovereignty

If populism is based on popular sovereignty, doesn't a defense of populism require a defense of popular sovereignty? Philosophically speaking, the answer is yes. But in the context of modern political debates, the answer is no, because in democratic debates, nobody gets anywhere by arguing against democracy. So in the political realm, the question is not "Why popular sovereignty?" but rather "Why *not* popular sovereignty?"

What would you say to a people whose sovereignty you wish to deny? You would have to tell them that they do not have the right to control their own affairs and pursue their own goals. Instead, they must do as you tell them because they must serve your ends, which are more important. Perhaps you wish to rule over them because their territory contains valuable resources that you wish to control. Perhaps you regard the people themselves as resources you wish to control. In short, you are telling them that you wish to make them slaves.

There is a real question if an *argument* is the appropriate response to such an unvarnished declaration of hostility. When someone declares you to be merely a tool for his own ends, he should not be surprised if you reach for your revolver.

But none of the critics of populism are this brazen, not even Bernard-Henri Lévy. Liberalism triumphed not by rejecting popular sovereignty but by subverting it. This is one reason the elites are so hysterical about the rise of populism. It puts them on the spot. If they affirm popular sovereignty, then populism is the only logical outcome. If they deny popular sovereignty, good luck getting people to vote for that. Thus they'd rather avoid the argument entirely. But we can't let them. We need to press this advantage by demanding that they live up to the principle of popular sovereignty, which empowers the people they loathe. In a fair contest, illiberal democracy will beat undemocratic liberalism every time.

Counter-Currents, August 27, 2020

National Populism Is Here to Stay*

The Revolt Against Globalism

According to the Left, the peoples of the world are about to join hands and step together into a new age of global government and multicultural harmony under the rule of benevolent, cosmopolitan elites. But there has been a little bump on the road to utopia, namely the rise of national populism: Brexit, Trump, Orbán, Salvini, the Yellow Vests, etc.

But many establishment voices assure us that these are just temporary setbacks. National populism is merely a matter of a few charismatic demagogues who popped up out of nowhere. Or it's merely the aftermath of the 2008 economic crisis, although that is more than a decade old. Or it is just a temporary reaction to the migrant crisis.

But, they insist, demagogues come and go. The old, white, male voters who put them in office are going to die soon, and they're going to be replaced by tolerant, open-minded Millennials and Zoomers and, of course, non-whites. Once non-white immigrants replace all these uppity problematic white people, we won't have to worry about populist demagogues anymore.

I guess they also think there will be no more sudden mass movements of people. Nor will there be any more economic crises. Emmanuel Macron was supposed to be the centrist, globalist answer to national populism, and that didn't work out exactly as planned. But still, they as-

---

* This is F.K.'s transcript of an extemporaneous lecture at the Etnofutur Conference in Tallinn, Estonia on February 25, 2019. It has been heavily edited and augmented. I wish to thank the organizers for inviting me to speak.

sure us that the march toward global liberal democracy will be back on track any day now.

I want to argue that the globalists are wrong. National populism is not a flash in the pan. National populism is the wave of the future, and ethnonationalists can surf that wave to power and influence.

EATWELL & GOODWIN'S *NATIONAL POPULISM*

I highly recommend the book *National Populism: The Revolt Against Liberal Democracy* by two British political scientists, Roger Eatwell and Matthew Goodwin.[1] There has been a spate of recent books on the threat of populism to liberal democracy. I thought *National Populism* was going to be just another book saying that there's nothing more threatening to democracy than listening to the will of the people. But I am pleased to report that I was completely wrong.

Although Eatwell and Goodwin are clearly men of the Left, they are also clearly *anti-liberal* men of the Left. Thus they have no patience for liberal cant about national populism. So they open their book by relentlessly tearing down liberal delusions about the imminent demise of national populism. They marshal some impressive empirical studies that indicate that national populism is here to stay; it is the result of a number of social and political trends in Europe and the United States. These trends are deep-seated, going back several decades, and they show no sign of abating any time in the near future.

One of the most amazing statistics they cite is from the World Values Survey. In Europe and the United States, an average of 82% of respondents say that "they feel strongly attached to their nation." An average of 93% "see them-

---

[1] Roger Eatwell and Matthew Goodwin, *National Populism: The Revolt Against Liberal Democracy* (New York: Pelican, 2018).

selves as part of their nation." An average of 90% "would be willing to fight for their nation" (p. 146). Those are remarkable numbers, and they indicate that we're not about to leap into globalism any time soon.

Eatwell and Goodwin also cite polls about attitudes towards European identity in the European Union: 71% of the elites in the EU feel that they benefit from the European Union, whereas only 34% of the overall population in EU countries feel that way (p. 104). Among EU elites, 50% believe that politicians don't care what the people think, whereas that figure is nearly 75% among the general public (p. 104). More than 70% of politicians in the European Union say that they feel very strongly about their European identity. Only about 50% of Europeans in general say they feel very strongly about their European identity (p. 101).

I'd wager that some people who feel strongly about their European identity are ethnonationalists, but we don't mean it in quite the same way that EU boosters do. It would also be interesting to learn what percentage of people like the EU for "Last Man" reasons, e.g., a single currency and passport-free travel make for better shopping. Finally, it would be interesting to know what percentage of those who like the EU do so because they regard it as an instrument of coercively imposing Left-wing values.

Eatwell and Goodwin analyze four factors that they think are contributing to national populism. They call them "the Four Ds." The first is *Distrust*, namely the breakdown of public trust in government. The second is *Destruction*, specifically the destruction of identity, the destruction of the ethnic composition and order of societies due to immigration and multiculturalism. The third trend is *Deprivation*, referring to the collapse of First World living standards—especially middle-class and working-class living standards—due to globalization. The final trend is *Dealignment*, meaning the abandonment of the center-Left, center-Right duopolies common in post-World War II democracies.

Distrust

Why does distrust contribute to populism? Populism is based on the distinction between the people, who have legitimate interests that are not being represented, and the corrupt governing elites, who serve their own interests—or foreign and minority interests—at the expense of the people.

We believe that government is legitimate if it governs in our legitimate interests. We believe that a government is more likely to govern in our interests if it is composed of people like us. In other words, we believe that self-government is real if we are governed by people like ourselves.

When our governing elites are conspicuously different from us, we don't trust them to govern in our interests; we expect them to govern in their own interests. When we arrive at that conclusion, the government no longer has legitimacy and needs to be replaced.

Legitimacy is important because if the state is not seen as legitimate, it cannot secure compliance with its policies without coercing the people. Coercion makes government costlier and further lowers its legitimacy.

Some of Eatwell and Goodwin's statistics illustrating distrust are quite remarkable. In 1964, 67% of Americans trusted the US government "most of the time." In 2012, when Barack Obama was re-elected president, that number had fallen to 22% (p. 121).

Another revealing poll is in answer to the statement "Political rulers don't care about people like me." In Sweden, 45% agreed with that statement. In Germany it was 52%; in the UK, 58%; the United States, 67%; Poland, 71%; Italy, 72%; France, 78%. Now, the global average of people who agree with that question is 63%, and the global average contains all manner of Third World kleptocracies, dictatorships, and failed states. So in Poland, Italy and France, there is significantly more distrust than the global average, and the global average is very bad, when you think about the kinds of countries that are factored into it (p. 123).

Ethnonationalists want regime change. We want self-determination for all peoples. Thus we want to replace the entire globalist establishment, Left and Right, with a new political establishment that puts the interests of each nation first. To do that, we must exploit and intensify the existing tendency towards distrust of the establishment. And we're already doing a pretty good job of that by:

- Emphasizing the differences—of ethnicity, culture, values, income, and especially interests—between the establishment and the people
- Emphasizing the similarities of the establishment in terms of their commitments to globalism, multiculturalism, immigration, Zionism, military interventionism, neoliberalism, sexual liberation, feminism, and cultural Leftism—as opposed to the people's desires for social conservatism, economic populism, and peace
- Exposing the establishment's lies, secretiveness, and lack of transparency, which are necessary to impose unpopular policies
- Exposing elite clubbishness, snobbery, and contempt for the people
- Exposing the hypocrisy of elites, who seek to exempt themselves and their children from the diversity they impose on the people
- Exposing the elites' systematic betrayal of the popular will, e.g., the refusal to deliver Brexit, the failure to enforce border security in the US,

the EU's refusal to abide by popular referenda if they deliver the "wrong" answer, etc.

- Exposing the simple corruption of political elites, who take bribes and contributions from special interests—including foreign governments—to betray the interests of the people
- To build a multicultural utopia, you've got to break a few eggs. Populists need to expose the catastrophic consequences of immigration and multiculturalism. Then we need to expose the establishment coverups of these same consequences.

Nationalists are really quite masterful at ferreting out, exposing, and mocking such things, contributing mightily to the de-legitimization and the distrust of our current elites. We need to keep it up.

But one word of caution: We can't go full Alex Jones. I think Alex Jones is a reckless liar who promotes conspiracies that he knows to be false because he wants to undermine people's trust in the social system. Every shooting is fake. Every terrorist attack is a false flag. We are asked to believe there are whole armies of "crisis actors." The state is so clever, wealthy, and powerful that it can create a completely fake image of reality.

If people believe such stories, it doesn't just lower their trust in the system, it lowers their trust in logic and their own lying eyes. But there's a problem with that. Complete epistemological nihilism is very easy to start, but it is hard to stop. You might think the nihilist train will take you to your destination, but when you pull the cord to make it stop, it's just going to keep barreling on down the tracks.

Such theories also presuppose that the system is basically all-powerful, which leads sensible people to the conclusion that resistance is futile. Frankly, if I were a corrupt and degenerate establishment with no hope of restoring social trust, I would promote people like Jones, because a society where there is zero social trust—even among the people—is a society unable to unite to overthrow its leadership.

What we need is *targeted* distrust. We need to target our leaders, but we cannot do so by telling lies that undermine people's ability to believe us or one another. We can't undermine public rationality—which is never too strong in the best of circumstances—or basic social cohesion, because we're going to need them. So we have to be truthful and scrupulous in our propaganda.

There are a lot of cynical people on the Right who have an almost cargo-cult mentality; they think they can overthrow our dishonest elites by becoming a dishonest elite of their own. They say, "The establishment lies to us all the time. Why can't we tell lies?" But we need to guard our credibility, because that's the greatest asset that we have. So propaganda: yes. Lies: no.

Destruction

Why does the destruction of identity through multiculturalism and immigration promote national populism? Quite simply because multiculturalism and immigration are imposed by elites on the populace. The working and middle classes suffer the most from immigration and multiculturalism, because they lack the money to insulate themselves from depressed wages and destroyed living spaces. National populists, however, promise to restrict immigration and preserve distinct national identities from multicultural erosion.

Eatwell and Goodwin cite a number of statistics that indicate that whites are increasingly resistant to demographic replacement and thus increasingly open to national populist messages. Right before the Brexit referendum, 48% of people in Great Britain said that the biggest political problem was immigration (p. 148). That is an extremely high number. In the United States, that number has never gone above 19% (p. 147).

Here's a poll answering the question: "Does immigration have a positive impact?" In Great Britain, 40% say that, but 45% also say that there are too many immigrants in the country, and 43% say that "immigration is causing my country to change in ways I don't like." In Canada, 40% are saying "immigration is changing the country in ways I don't like." In the United States it's 46%, in Sweden 44%, in Spain 46%, in Germany 45%, in Poland 41%. They have a tiny amount of immigration in Poland, but they're very sensitive about it, which is a good sign. France: 49%, Belgium: 56%, Italy: 63%, and Hungary: 54% (p. 149).

They cite an Ipsos-MORI survey from after Trump's election revealing that only one in four Americans felt that immigration was good for the country; in France, that number was 14%, in Italy 10%, in Hungary 5% (p. 277).

They also cite a poll about people's willingness to have a complete ban on Muslim immigration (p. 155): In Poland, 71% are for it, and only 9% would oppose it. In Austria, 65% would want a complete ban on Muslim immigration, and only 18% oppose it. In Hungary: 64%, Belgium: 64%, France: 61%, Greece: 58%, Germany: 53%, Italy: 51%, the United Kingdom: 47%, Spain: 41%. After Alternative for Germany made electoral breakthroughs, 60% of Germans told pollsters that Islam had no place in their country (p. 277). Poland and Hungary have the lowest numbers of people who would oppose a ban on Muslim immigration and among the highest numbers of people who would support it. I am not seeing a lot of openness to radical multiculturalism in these numbers.

Surprisingly, the authors argue that there is nothing immoral *per se* about wanting to preserve the ethnic identity of one's society (pp. 74–78). That is an astonishing concession from men of the Left. They also argue that for many people it is simply common sense to want to preserve a society where they feel at home and to feel that we have greater obligations to our neighbors and countrymen than to strangers. Naturally, very large numbers of people resent it when Leftists accuse them of being racists over such common-sense attitudes (pp. 78, 161–62).

Eatwell and Goodwin also cite studies indicating that significant numbers of people reject the idea that economic performance is the sole standard of national well-being. For instance, when asked whether "strong community and family life is as important to well-being as a strong economy," 78% of Americans, 79% of Britons, and 83% of Germans agreed (p. 217).

Even in the proverbial "land of shopkeepers," a very significant number of pro-Brexit voters believed that identity is more important than economics, whereas the anti-Brexit crowd was predicting Biblical plagues, economic collapse, and so forth if Brexit won.

A lot of people didn't believe such predictions. But some felt that even if they were true, it would be worth it to get their national sovereignty back, which is quite remarkable. For instance, 60% of Britons said that "significant damage to the British economy would be a 'price worth paying for Brexit,'" and 40% were willing to see their own relatives lose jobs to secure Brexit (p. 36; cf. p. 278).

These are attitudes that ethnonationalists can build upon. Our movement has been working for decades to raise awareness of the destructiveness of ethnic change. But we can't congratulate ourselves too much, for our efforts to raise consciousness pale by comparison to the effects of multiculturalism. We may be pulling some people in our direction, but multiculturalism itself is stampeding them toward us.

Thus I think our most important role is less in *raising* consciousness than in *deepening* consciousness. We have explanations of why multiculturalism creates alienation and conflict. We can explain who is behind globalization, immigration, and multiculturalism and why. We defend the moral legitimacy of white identity politics against the widespread notion that white identity politics, and *only* white identity politics, is immoral *per se*. That moral taboo is the great dam holding back the tide of national populism. If we can breach that dam, it will unleash the floodwaters of white identity. Finally, we can offer workable and humane alternatives, not just Right-wing civic nationalism, which basically is just lying about diversity in a different way.

Deprivation

It's really simple to deepen people's understanding of deprivation due to globalization. All it requires is elementary economics. Globalization means creating a single world market for labor and goods. A global labor market means that working- and middle-class wages and living standards in the First World will drop quite a bit, and wages and living standards in the Third World will rise a little bit, until we reach a global average which will represent the pauperization of all advanced industrial societies, East and West. But global economic elites will grow very rich indeed as they pauperize the First World.[2]

Because the disastrous consequences of globalization can be predicted by basic economics, globalization could never have been put to a vote. The vast majority of First Worlders would not vote to pauperize themselves. Thus globalization had to be imposed by elites using every possible subterfuge. Thus to reverse globalization, national populists need to overthrow the existing elites and institute protectionist economic policies. We need to reindustrialize the First World.

---

[2] Greg Johnson, "The End of Globalization," *Truth, Justice, & a Nice White Country* (San Francisco: Counter-Currents, 2015).

Dealignment

Dealignment is basically the breakdown of the post-World War II political system in which power was traded between center-Left and center-Right parties, while Western societies drifted steadily toward cultural Leftism, bigger and more intrusive government, and the loss of sovereignty to globalization.

The 2017 French presidential election is a remarkable example of dealignment. The final showdown did not include the center-Left or center-Right candidates, but instead far-Rightist Marine Le Pen and far-globalist Emanuel Macron. Of course, Macron was simply a rebranded Socialist candidate, but the fact remains that the Socialist Party's credibility was so damaged that a rebrand was necessary.

An even more striking example is the 2019 European Parliament elections in the UK, in which Nigel Farage's newly-created Brexit Party won more than 30% of the vote. Labour lost half of its seats. The Tories lost 75% of their seats. And the Liberal Democrats went from one to sixteen seats, simply because some disaffected Labour and Tory voters would not vote for the Brexit Party.

These elections are like an American presidential contest in which the two main candidates are neither Democrats nor Republicans. They represent remarkable changes in political alignments and loyalties in France and the UK.

The main factor behind dealignment is the increasing realization on the part of voters that there aren't really any fundamental differences between the parties. There is no real competition. Instead, there is a political cartel. There is a political establishment that has different fronts. The different branches of the establishment agree on all important matters. They disagree only on inessential matters, as a kind of theater that captivates the public and keeps them both politically engaged and politically divided.

A lot of people naïvely think that political power primarily means beating the other team in political contests, like elections. But there's a deeper form of political power that determines all the things that the parties *don't* fight about and that are never put to the choice of the voters. That's *real* power. That's the power to *frame* all political debates in a way that makes them safe for the existing establishment.

Ethnonationalists are very good at unmasking the cartelized, fake nature of democratic politics. The political establishment is an exclusive club, and a politician can only join if he swears to represent the interests of the elites as opposed to the voters who actually elect him. Election after election, the people send their tribunes to the capitals, only to see them absorbed by the establishment. Thus when there is a conflict between the public interest and elite interests, it is impossible to believe that our representatives will side with the public.

The shameful refusal of the Tories to deliver Brexit is spectacular proof of that. Theresa May had one job as Prime Minister: to deliver Brexit. She did not do it, because she did not *want* to do it, because the global elites did not want it to happen. Once people see through the charade of the current party system, they will realize that their sovereignty is being systematically negated. Then radical new political alignments become possible.

What kind of government do most white people want? We want a socially conservative, interventionist state, a state that takes the side of the working and middle classes against the elites, and a state that takes the side of citizens against foreigners. They want a mixed economy, not pure capitalism or pure socialism.

Interestingly enough, even in the United States, where Koch brothers-funded, libertarian economics is a dogma amongst Republican politicians and pundits, many Republican voters are very much opposed to dismantling social safety nets. According to Eatwell and Goodwin, 73% of Trump voters were opposed to touching entitlement programs and social safety nets. They were even more opposed than some Bernie Sanders and Hillary Clinton voters (p. 264).

But the elites want a very different form of government. If the people want a socially conservative, interventionist state, the elites want a socially liberal, globalist oligarchy. Thus they want to dismantle all the barriers that stand in their way: tariffs, borders, unions, national identities and attachments, etc. Jonathan Bowden called this global neoliberal system "Left-wing oligarchy," a marriage of Leftist values and hyper-stratified, oligarchical capitalism.[3]

Americans want a socially conservative interventionist state. But we are never allowed to simply vote for what we really want. The Republicans will say: "We stand for conservative values!" But they package them with neoliberal economics. The Democrats say: "We stand for an interventionist state!" But they package it with social degeneracy.

When the Democrats get into power, they give the elites what they want: more social degeneracy. But they don't touch neoliberal economic policies, because that's also what the elites want. When the Republicans are in power, they give tax cuts to oligarchs, but they don't deliver on the really important issues, like building a border wall, because the oligarchs don't want that any more than they want social conservatism.

Thus no matter who is in power, the elites get what they want, and the people don't. Thus politics and society drift further and further toward Left-wing oligarchy.

Contemporary representative democracy also thrives

---

[3] Jonathan Bowden, "The Essence of the Left," *Counter-Currents*, August 26, 2016.

on negative legitimization. The Democrats in America say: "Vote for us, because we're not those horrible Republicans!" And the Republicans say: "Vote for us, because we're not those horrible Democrats!" People get elected into power, based not on what they represent, or even on who they are, but on who they are *not*. This gives them a blank check to do whatever they want when they are in office, so long as they are sufficiently unlike their hated enemies. And, through some strange coincidence, they always find it easier to go along with the establishment agenda of social liberalism and global oligarchy.

When Donald Trump was elected, he struck terror into the hearts of the elites. But what has he done as President? Everything the oligarchy loves: typical Republican policies. But he has not built a border wall. That is very telling. It is the same old pattern. Western liberal democracy thrives on giving the people all sorts of choices, except what we really want. Unmasking this pattern contributes a great deal to political dealignment and the rise of national populism.

Riding the Wave

Eatwell and Goodwin have a great wave on the cover of their book because they believe national populism is the wave of the future. They actually go so far as to predict, in the chapter called "The Post-Populist Moment?," that there won't be a post-populist moment.

The only way establishment parties will be able to compete with national populism is to adopt national populist policies. Maybe water them down, lighten them up a bit: national populism lite. But that is a very important admission, because it means that the hegemony of globalism is over. Instead of debating about different forms of globalism, we will now be debating about different forms of national populism. That creates an opportunity for ethnonationalists to enter political debates and win.

So how do we surf this wave?

First, what do we bring to the table? Ethnonationalists have the most realistic understanding of what nations and peoples are, and what makes them flourish or fail. Based on history, social science, and ultimately biology, we argue that societies are strengthened by genetic and cultural homogeneity and weakened by genetic and cultural diversity.[4]

Populism means that the people are sovereign. National populism means that the sovereign people is a nation. But what is a nation? Our answer is that a nation is primarily an extended family united by a common history, language, and culture, i.e., an ethnic group.

A secondary component of a nation consists of outsiders who have been "naturalized," i.e., who have become part of the nation through intermarriage and cultural assimilation. Ethnonationalists hold that it is the right of the nation in the primary sense to determine who can be naturalized, and how many. If a nation wishes to preserve and propagate itself through time, it needs to keep naturalizations to a small number of people, and these people need to be as racially and culturally similar as possible to the original population.

Thus we reject the "civic nationalist" idea that just anyone—much less untold millions of culturally and racially diverse people—can become part of a nation simply by swearing allegiance to a national creed. Civic nationalism, by ignoring the destructive effects of genetic and cultural diversity, is a prescription for alienation and conflict.

Second, to ride the national populist wave, we must be *genuine* national populists. That means that we need to curtail and discard some features of the contemporary

---

[4] See Greg Johnson, "What's Wrong with Diversity?" and "Homogeneity" in *The White Nationalist Manifesto* and *It's Okay to Be White*.

ethnonationalist movement, namely anti-populist forms of elitism and residual free-market liberalism.

There are a lot of genuinely anti-populist ideas floating around the ethnonationalist Right. Many people sneer at the very idea of popular sovereignty, claiming instead that sovereignty should reside in dynasties or priesthoods or elites, not peoples. Others sneer at the idea of democracy. All of these ideas are self-marginalizing and self-defeating.

According to Eatwell and Goodwin, "most national-populist voters want *more* democracy—*more* referendums and *more* empathetic and listening politicians that give *more* power to the people and less power to established economic and political elites" (pp. xi-xii). We will not capture the allegiance of such people by proposing a return to the Law of Manu.

It's easy to dismiss representative democracy, given how badly it works today. But as Alain de Benoist has pointed out, if we actually had direct democracy on issues like trade and immigration, we'd have much better policies.[5] If people could vote on matters of policy, day-by-day, with their smartphones, we'd have better outcomes than we get with representative democracy. That's a sobering truth.

In my essay "Notes on Populism, Elitism, and Democracy," I employ arguments from Aristotle's *Politics* to argue that an ethnostate should have a strong element of democracy.[6] The standard of justice is the common good of a people, and a genuine people is an ethnic group. To say that the common good of a people is the standard of justice is equivalent to saying that the people is sovereign.

---

[5] Alain de Benoist, *The Problem of Democracy* (London: Arktos, 2011).

[6] Greg Johnson, "Notes on Populism, Elitism, and Democracy," *New Right vs. Old Right*; "Introduction to Aristotle's *Politics*," *From Plato to Postmodernism*.

However, the people's common good is an objective reality. It is not something that can be determined simply by convention. Therefore, government deliberations do not *create* the common good; they *discover* it. Because it is possible for the majority to be wrong about the common good, simply voting is not enough to determine what it is. The common good can only be discovered by rational inquiry. But some people are more rational than others, and the most rational people constitute a small elite.

However, if the determination of the common good is left only to the few, there is a danger that they will pursue their own elite interests at the expense of the body politic. Therefore, to secure the common good, the people need to have a voice.

Thus we are more likely to serve the common good if we have a regime with both aristocratic (elitist) and popular (democratic) elements, in which the elites can guide the masses toward the truth about the common good, and the masses can deter the elites from ruling at the expense of the common good. Both the elites and the masses need to participate if we are to have genuinely populist government.

Rightists reject the idea that equality is the highest political good. Some on the Right go so far as to make inequality and hierarchy into the highest good. My answer to them is: What kind of hierarchy? Just hierarchies or unjust hierarchies? There can be good hierarchies and bad hierarchies. There can be good and bad, just and unjust, forms of inequality. We should stand for justice. Not hierarchy as such: a *just* hierarchy. Not inequality as such: a *just* inequality.

And if our primary focus is justice, there's a lot to be said for democracy, rightly understood. Ethnonationalists can get almost everything we want simply by perfecting democracy. But we get absolutely nowhere by making a fetish out of inequality and hierarchy.

National populists also need to genuinely embrace economic interventionism. There is a tendency for people on the Right to embrace free-market economic policies that are subversive of the common good and out of sync with what people want, even in the United States, the country most inclined toward free-market capitalism.

Economics is a genuine science, but most of our people believe that identity is more important than economic efficiency. Our people believe that protecting national sovereignty and flourishing working and middle classes from globalization is more important than free trade. We need to bow to these preferences. These are questions of political values that cannot be settled by economics as such.

There is obviously much more to be said about how ethnonationalists can better align ourselves with national populism. The first thing we need to do is understand it. Thus I highly recommend Eatwell and Goodwin's *National Populism* to all the big brains in our movement. It's not the final say on these matters, but it's a necessary first step.

Beyond that, I think we have to recognize that we're entering an age of great unpredictability and instability. Times like these are quite resistant to grand designs, to people who think they can figure out how it's all going to unfold. For instance, when Eatwell and Goodwin wrote their book, the Yellow Vests didn't exist. What a surprise that was! Although looking at Eatwell and Goodwin's numbers about the extremely high level of distrust in the establishment in France, it makes sense that the Yellow Vests happened there.

If history is full of surprises, what do we do? Let's look at the Yellow Vests. It was very much a spontaneous, populist uprising. It was nobody's grand design. But certain things made it possible. First is the absolute saturation of French society with nationalist and populist ideas. You can't go anywhere in France without being exposed to national populist critiques of and alternatives to the current system. Every French person knows about the problems with globalization and immigration. Second are the social networks that allowed people to organize and propagate these protests very quickly and sustain them for months on end.

But fostering ideas and social networks that make political change possible is the task of New Right metapolitics. It is what we are doing right now. So we need to do more of the same, but thanks to Eatwell and Goodwin, we can do so with renewed confidence that our efforts are aligned with deep-seated, long-lasting social trends. There is a great wave rising up behind us, a wave that might carry us, finally, to our goals.

Counter-Currents, July 16, 2019

UPPITY WHITE FOLKS & HOW TO REACH THEM*

AFTER *THE WHITE NATIONALIST MANIFESTO*

This is the sixth time that I've spoken in Sweden, which practically makes me a migrant. I keep getting invited to Sweden because I have a lot of readers here. In terms of *Counter-Currents* readers, the top country every month is the United States. Then usually you have the other major countries of the Anglosphere—the UK, Canada, and Australia—plus France and Germany trading spots in the top six. And then, after that, down around number seven you usually find Sweden. Sweden is a country of nine million white people. But it's an honorary Anglosphere country because you all speak and read English so well. So it didn't really surprise me that we had a lot of readers here. So I started developing friends and contacts here, and that's what's led me here all these times.

Sweden has also distinguished itself by being the country where my books have been translated first and most often. *The White Nationalist Manifesto* is my third book translated into Swedish. My first translation into any language was the Swedish edition of *New Right vs. Old Right*. *Truth, Justice, and a Nice White Country* came out next. That is the first and only translation of that book into a foreign language. And this is the first translation of my *Manifesto*.

---

* The following text is an extensively revised transcript of my talk in Gothenburg, Sweden, on Sunday, September 22, 2019, on the occasion of the publication of the Swedish translation of *The White Nationalist Manifesto*. I want to thank Pál Csató for the transcript as well as my Swedish hosts and audience.

The *Manifesto* came out almost exactly one year ago. I've just put out a new edition of it in English; we now have the Swedish translation; there is a Ukrainian translation in the works; there is a fellow working on a Portuguese translation; German, Spanish, Norwegian, Dutch, and Polish translations are underway; and I'm looking to get translations done into French and Italian. Eventually, I would love to see it in every European language. But the Swedes were first. You guys are at the vanguard, and I very much appreciate that. So give yourselves a hand.

Once the *Manifesto* was done, I didn't want to look at it for a while. When I prepared the second edition back in August, I read through it again, for the first time in a year. I found some typos that stabbed me in the heart. How did these things get through? There was also a mistake in the index. But I was pretty much satisfied with it.

I don't think this is the best case that could ever be made for white ethnonationalism. I'd like somebody else to come along and outdo it. But I feel it's the best case that *I* can make for this particular argument. I'm going to keep this book in print. I'm going to keep bringing out new editions, if I figure out ways of improving it. I'm going to pursue new translations.

My next big project, however, is to take into account all the changes that have happened in the world in the last year. Because in the year since this book was first published there have been some dramatic changes, not just in the political world, but in the intellectual world. I want to talk about those intellectual changes and how they would change the way I would write this book, if I were to write it again today.

I'm actually working on another book now called *White Identity Politics*. *White Identity Politics* takes into account some very useful books that have been published in the last year. I want to talk about a couple of these books and give you a roadmap of that project. I want to share this with you because I think what's happening is profoundly encouraging. This is a "white-pill" speech. I think there's a lot of reason for optimism in our cause.

A Modest Proposal

We're here because we are far-sighted people, because we are looking down the road and seeing ominous trends that must be changed. We don't like the future that's being prepared for us. We want to interrupt those plans. We want to create a better future.

Most people, however, are not far-sighted. Most people don't think many years ahead. That's why democracy is often a very bad political system. Democracy allows ambitious people to gain power by appealing to the masses. And the masses are always short-sighted. Thus people can gain power by proposing ideas that sound good in the short run but have disastrous long-term consequences, knowing that relatively few people can think ahead to the disastrous consequences. The far-sighted few are outvoted by the short-sighted many. That's the problem we face.

So one of the problems for us is *how to explain White Nationalism to short-sighted people*. People who only think a year or two ahead.

First of all, White Nationalism just means the independence, the ethnic self-determination of all European peoples in whatever homelands they have. So White Nationalism means Swedish nationalism in Sweden and Norwegian nationalism in Norway. That's all it means, as far as I'm concerned. So I am going to speak of Swedish nationalism while in Sweden, with the understanding that the same principles apply to all white peoples around the globe.

What does White Nationalism mean in Sweden? White Nationalism is the shocking, radical proposal for the state to ensure that next year the Swedish percentage of Sweden's population will be greater than it is this year, whereas the entire current establishment in Sweden—all the political parties—are committed to the position that next year there will be fewer Swedes in Sweden.

Imagine proposing the following to any Swedish politician. "The Swedish Arctic fox population has been steadily declining for a long time. If it continues to decline, at some point there will be no more Arctic foxes in Sweden. What policies do you propose to save the Arctic fox?"

I guarantee that not a single Swedish politician would simply say he doesn't care. A lot of them *don't* care. But they would never have the gall to *say* it. Nobody has to give reasons to save the Arctic fox. And nobody has the gall to argue against it.

Now if you were to propose the radical idea of political policies that will make sure that next year there will more Swedes in Sweden, and the year after that still more, is there any really good argument against that proposal?

Sweden isn't overpopulated, and we are not talking about increasing absolute numbers anyway, but simply the Swedish percentage of Sweden's population.

That's not the kind of proposal that an honest person can really oppose. The natural answer to a proposal like that is not "Why?" but "Why not?" Why wouldn't we want more Swedes in Sweden next year than there are this year? Why wouldn't we want the Swedish percentage of Sweden's population to be higher next year than it is this year?

If you put Swedish nationalism in those terms, it's what we call an easy sell. People are always saying, "Greg, you've got to tone it down a bit. White Nationalism is far too radical. It's very hard to sell people on the idea of a homeland named Sweden for the Swedes. That's very controversial and problematic these days."

But I honestly think that if you propose Swedish nationalism to people in these simple terms—we want more Swedes in Sweden—it's got to be the easiest sell possible.

The only reason to oppose it, frankly, is if you think

Sweden would be improved by fewer Swedes. If you hate Swedish people and want them to die, you'll want fewer Swedes in Sweden next year, and the year after that, and the year after that. Of course you want to blur the long term out, because the long-term trend means that eventually there'll be no Swedish people in Sweden.

There actually are evil-minded people who think Sweden would be improved by fewer Swedes. So just ask them whether they want Sweden to be more or less Swedish next year. Don't let them evade that question. It is good to get them on the record. It is also good to get politicians on the record about this question, because some of them actively promote such policies. Others just go along with them.

But few if any establishment voices will say that Sweden would be a better place by being more Swedish. And even then, you have to watch out, because one of the enemy's tricks is to say that Swedishness has nothing to do with ethnicity. It's all about tolerance and inclusion. They say the same thing about Englishness and Americanness. Basically, they want to redefine your identity as a willingness to be replaced by foreigners. If somebody defines you as replaceable, it is because he wants to replace you. But your identity is not to be a fool. Don't fall for that.

The project that I want to work on now is how to connect present-day political concerns with radical, fundamental, and long-term thinking about white extinction, white genocide, and how to create white homelands. The problems that we fear and the solutions we propose will happen in the far future. How do we relate to people as they are right now, especially short-sighted people who only think a couple of years down the road?

The good news is that there's quite a bit of evidence that our people are increasingly concerned about ethnic identity issues and ethnic displacement. We've been predicting for a very long time that as non-white immigration and race replacement grow, more and more people will become aware of it, and they'll want to stop it.

EATWELL & GOODWIN'S *NATIONAL POPULISM*

The first book I want to recommend to you is *National Populism: The Revolt Against Liberal Democracy* by two British academics, Roger Eatwell and Matthew Goodwin. It came out in November, 2018. I picked it up and added it to a stack of recent books on populism, thinking it would be another globalist establishment attack on national populism. And I was very pleased at how wrong I was about this book. Even though the authors are men of the Left, it's very clear they're not liberal. They're anti-liberal men of the Left. And they have a sympathy on some level for populism.

They see that liberal democracy, as it's practiced today, basically means minority rule. Liberal democratic elites make an art of never giving the public what they want. The people in every white society want a socially conservative state that will intervene in the economy to protect the working and middle classes. That is what national populists stand for. The elites want social liberalism and untrammeled global capitalism, what Jonathan Bowden described as Left-wing oligarchy.

A wonderful example of liberal democracy in action is the UK since the Brexit vote. The British people voted for Brexit out of patriotism and a desire for a more responsive government that puts the British people first. The British establishment is doing everything it possibly can to not give the people what they want. That's how post-war liberal democracy is structured in every white country around the world. It's a very clever system for not giving the people what they want.

People are becoming increasingly aware of this, and that's causing the rise of national populist parties, candidates, and initiatives all across the white world. Trump.

Brexit. These were huge shocks to the progressive liberal establishment. They really believe there's this thing called progress, that the arc of history bends in the direction of their wishes. And when Trump and Brexit came along, it shook them up. It suggested a very different narrative. If Brexit can happen, Trump can get elected. And if Trump can get elected, Marine Le Pen can get elected. And then it's all over!

So progressives came up with coping mechanisms, little stories they told to convince themselves that progress is going to be back really soon. One story they told themselves is that national populism is the last hurrah of angry old white people, especially white men, who are going to die off and be replaced by tolerant Millennials and vibrant non-whites, who will vote like liberal democrats want them to vote.

When progressives say that, it's a vision of utopia. When we say that, it's a "conspiracy theory" called the "Great Replacement." The Left's brilliant plan is to fill white countries with Muslims and Africans and Mestizos, and then we will see the final triumph of liberalism. Gay marriage, feminism, abortion rights, kindness to animals and trees, walkable communities, green energy, and universal health care will finally be secured by a Third World majority. Of course, none of these things are valued in the Third World, but the rising non-white majority will always vote like the ever-dwindling population of white liberals wants them to. So we're going to finally triumph over the forces of reaction and have our liberal utopia. It's a highly delusional and questionable plan. But that's the plan.

In America, the plan is to create a Scandinavian-style Social Democratic utopia—not by filling the country with Scandinavians, who have created such societies, but by filling it with Mexicans, who have created only kleptocratic dystopias.

Eatwell and Goodwin argue that globalization will not

get back on track any time soon, and that all the liberal coping is based on false premises. They argue that the trend towards national populism is not just a momentary glitch. Rather, it is a product of some long-term, deep-seated trends in all white societies. They call these trends the four Ds: Distrust, Destruction, Deprivation, and De-alignment. They are the Four Horsemen of the liberal Apocalypse.

Distrust by the people of the establishment has been growing tremendously in every white society. Populism is premised on the people distrusting the elites, feeling like the elites are disconnected and pursuing their own interests at the expense of the people. If you believe that, you're a populist. And the number of people who believe that thesis grows every year, and it has been growing every year for decades now.

There's no sign that the trend toward distrust is going to change, because people are increasingly aware that the establishment really doesn't represent their interests, that it's out of touch, that it's contemptuous of the electorate, and that it wants a future where we have no future. The people will not suddenly get dumber overnight and go back to trusting the establishment—unless, of course, the establishment actually changes their policies and becomes populist. But they are bound and determined *not* to change their policies. They want to double down on their policies. Since the same causes give rise to the same effects, we can expect rising popular distrust well into the future.

Destruction refers to the results of immigration and multiculturalism. Eatwell and Goodwin admit that diversity is destructive. Many white people are experiencing that. They see that the societies they will die in will be utterly alien, ethnically speaking, to the societies they were born in. Increasingly, they are drawing the conclusion that this is wrong. A lot of people want to grow old and die in a country that somewhat resembles the country they grew up in.

Interestingly enough, Eatwell and Goodwin defend the idea that there's nothing wrong with that. It doesn't make you a bad person to want to preserve the character of your society, including the ethnic character of your society, for yourself and for future generations. That's what it is to have a homeland.

Now, what's the first thing that Leftists will accuse you of if you say such things? Racism! They always go straight for the racism charge. And large numbers of people are very indignant when that happens. They don't think there's anything bad or racist about wanting to preserve one's country from dramatic ethnic and cultural change. This is a growing consensus, and the racism word isn't inhibiting people.

These people still believe that racism is a really bad thing, and they don't want to be racist. But they don't think they *are* racist, and so they're quite angry when people call them this bad word, and say they are bad people with bad thoughts.

This suggests another way we can formulate our politics. Swedish nationalism is the view that the country you die in should be like the country you grew up in; that when you die, you're not going to be surrounded by strangers—by thieving, abusive people from other cultures, who just want you to die and get out of the way. Swedish nationalism is the view that Swedes should preserve a homeland that they actually feel at home in, and pass a similar blessing on to future generations.

We aren't opposed to technological change, although it is not always a blessing. Things that can be improved, should be improved. But feeling at home in one's homeland is not a problem, and multiculturalism is not a solution. Multiculturalism causes alienation, mistrust, and the breakdown of society. Beyond that, one of the things white countries have lost through multiculturalism is precisely their technological optimism.[1]

Deprivation just means the destruction of working-class and middle-class living standards in white countries by globalization: sending factories and jobs overseas, bringing cheap labor here. The destruction of working-class and middle-class incomes in the First World is a trend going back to the 1970s. Many of you never lived in a society where the average Joe, the average working person, could expect a better future than his parents. A lot of people are getting really angry about that and are increasingly receptive to populist anti-globalization messages. This is especially true of the Millennials and Gen-Zers, who will supposedly vote progressives back into power when angry old white populists die off.

Dealignment simply means that people are no longer going to vote for the center-Left or center-Right option. Post-war politics in the white world is basically the following system: You've got a center-Left party and a center-Right party that trade power occasionally with one another. They will compete on issues like abortion or taxes. But there are certain things that they agree not to compete on. They have agreed not to compete on multiculturalism, immigration, and economic globalization. No matter what party you choose, they're going to give you more multiculturalism, more immigration, and more globalization.

The most revolutionary thing that Donald Trump did in 2015, when he glided down the golden escalator at Trump Tower and announced that he was running for President of the United States, is that he broke that cartel, that gentlemen's agreement not to compete on immigration and globalization. He didn't have to do that. He could

---

[1] See Greg Johnson, "Technological Utopianism and Ethnic Nationalism" in *Toward a New Nationalism* and *It's Okay to Be White*.

have still won his party's nomination and the presidency by following the rules and not competing on those issues. He chose to compete on those issues, and therefore he had to fight a two-front war against the Democratic Party and his own party, to get the presidency.

That was revolutionary, because it showed that there are large numbers of people—sixty-plus million people in the United States—who really would vote for a nationalist candidate, a candidate who had an America-first foreign policy, was anti-globalization, and was anti-immigration. That was terrifying to the establishment. He broke the gentlemen's agreement. He broke the political cartel that's been in place since the Second World War.

Now we see this dealignment happening all over Europe. In the last French presidential election, we had Marine Le Pen—the far-Right candidate, the national populist candidate—against Emanuel Macron. Macron was presented as a political "outsider." He is actually an insider. He was a minister in the Socialist government who broke with them, ran as a "maverick," and got elected. Why the charade of having a socialist run as an independent? Because the Socialist Party was cooked. They had so little credibility after Hollande that the only way they could win was to put up this Macron character, this fake populist, this synthetic maverick. They had to run an establishment candidate as an anti-establishment candidate. The last French presidential election was as revolutionary and shocking as an American presidential election where there's no Democrat and no Republican in the final running.

People are leaving the center-Left/center-Right charade behind. They realize it *is* a charade. They realize it's a way of controlling the populace. They realize it's a way of not giving the people what they want. But democracy should be about giving the people what they want. When you actually get rumblings of real democracy, people call that "populism," and they write ridiculous books, like Yascha Mounk's *The People vs. Democracy*, on the terrible threat of populism.

Not only do Eatwell and Goodwin claim that national populism is based on deep-seated trends that go back decades and will go on well into the future, they argue that establishment parties will only be able to hold on to power by adopting national populist policies. Which means that globalization as the dominant political model is over, and that nationalism and populism are the future. That's a very encouraging message. It's a surprising message for a couple of Left-of-center British political scientists. But I find it very convincing. So we need to figure out how to use Eatwell and Goodwin's research to connect with the rising tide of national populism.

Ashley Jardina's *White Identity Politics*

Another book that I want to recommend is Ashley Jardina's *White Identity Politics*.[2] I was intending to write a book of the same title, and guess what, I still am. You can't copyright titles, so my *White Identity Politics* book will someday eclipse her *White Identity Politics* book. I'm also going to write a book called *The Great Replacement*, because why not? It's a great title and a great meme.

Jardina looks at polls that have been done of the American electorate over a seven-year period. The numbers are not extremely high: between around 800 to 1,200 white people polled. But they're high enough for valid social science conclusions. I find her results very encouraging.

We've been predicting for a long time that as white dispossession increases, white racial identity will also increase. When whites feel like they're running everything and are not threatened, it's easy to think that we're not

---

[2] Ashley Jardina, *White Identity Politics* (Cambridge: Cambridge University Press, 2019).

even really a racialized group. We're just human beings. And all the other human beings want to be just like us. That's the default liberal assumption: that we don't even belong to a race or a group. We're just *humanity*. And everybody else wants to be just like us. It's a deeply ethnocentric, supremacist attitude, but that's really the liberal attitude—in this country and in America as well.

You would only expect people like that to become racially aware if their sense of being secure and simply representing humanity was somewhat challenged. And of course it's being challenged. It's being challenged by diversity. It's being challenged by people complaining that even white liberals are racists. The people who don't see race are now racists, too. There's no redemption anymore. Even if you are a white liberal who does everything possible to help out non-whites, they'll still say you're a racist. I encourage this attitude, because it's making more whites race-aware, and it is driving people away from the liberal universalist paradigm towards a more racialized consciousness.

I want to look at four questions on racial attitudes discussed by Jardina.

The first question is about the importance of white racial identity to Americans today. The top two categories are the people who think that racial identity is *very important* or *extremely important* to them. And if you add those two numbers up, between 28% and 42% of Americans say that their racial identity is very important or extremely important to them. Now if you add in the people saying it's *moderately* important to them, you get 52% to 73% of white Americans saying that their racial identity is moderately to extremely important to them (p. 63).

Now that's very interesting. If you compare it with blacks, however, it's kind of sobering. The number of blacks who say that their racial identity is *very important* or *extremely important* is 69% to 85% in the same polls, which means more than double the white rate. And the number of blacks who say that their race is *extremely important* to them, just that alone ranges from 45% to 61% (p. 64). Racial identity is far more important to black Americans than it is to white Americans. But the fact remains that more white Americans now than in decades past are saying that their racial identity is important to them.

Another question is about pride in one's race. Do whites think they have a lot to be proud of? Again the numbers in the various polls range from between 30% and 40% of whites saying that they think they have *a lot to be proud of* or *quite a lot to be proud of*, which are the top two categories (p. 65). Those numbers should be a lot higher, of course, given the objective achievements of our race. But given that the entire culture and educational system are devoted to inculcating white guilt and denigrating white achievements, these numbers are encouraging.

The number of people who respond positively to the statement that they believe that whites are being discriminated against by the system in America is quite interesting. The system includes business, academia, the political establishment, and so forth. The number of people who *deny* that white people are being discriminated against by the American system today—which we are told by Leftists is a system of "white privilege"—the number of people who *believe* in white privilege is anywhere from 14% to 25% (p. 67). That means that 86% to 75% of Americans believe that white privilege is not a real thing, and in fact it's just the opposite, that whites are being penalized in America today.

The number of whites who believe that it is a good thing for us to collectivize and organize to protect white interests is also remarkably high. The people who say that white political mobilization is *not* necessary range from 16% to 23% (pp. 67–68). That means that 84% to 77% of white Americans believe that it is okay, and maybe a good thing to one degree or another, for whites to collectivize and organize to protect their interests.

What is it called when whites collectivize and organize to protect their interests? We call that white identity politics.

White identity politics ranges on a spectrum. On one end, there's what we call "implicit" white identity politics, which is basically what Republicans have been doing for a long time. They get white votes by proposing policies that "just so happen" to fit the political preferences of white people. But they always frame these policies as good for humanity or good for America. They don't explicitly court white people, but they will propose policies that white people regard positively.

On the other extreme is "explicit" white identity politics, which is what I'm arguing for in my *Manifesto* and everything else that I write.

Then there's a large and growing category in the middle. This is the category of people that the Republican Party doesn't want to touch explicitly. But again, between 84% and 77% of white Americans believe that it would be okay for whites to organize to protect their group interests. They're not necessarily envisioning White Nationalism, a white ethnostate, or an end to multiculturalism. But as long as there *is* multiculturalism, they're damn certain that whites have to take their own side in the ethnic conflicts that exist in multicultural societies. A very large number of people believe that. But the Republican Party will not appeal to them. They simply will not appeal explicitly to white interests, but very large numbers of whites believe that it would be perfectly legitimate if they did so.

I call these people in the middle "uppity white folks." They're not ready to be White Nationalists, and yet they *are* ready for white identity politics within the context of a multiracial, multicultural society. That's a huge number of people. That is where our movement can expect its growth. Thus the great task that faces us is to get inside the heads of those people.

From Identity to Identity Politics

I want to point out just one thing about their mentality that's very unusual according to Eatwell and Goodwin as well as Jardina. Jardina is especially useful because she actually has recent numbers that show that those Americans who have positive racial identity and are willing to countenance white identity politics *do not* significantly overlap with Americans who have negative attitudes about other races.

Let me repeat that. There's a large population that thinks well of being white and thinks that whites should look out for their interests. There's also a population of white Americans who have very negative views of other races. And those two sets *do not* significantly overlap. There's only a small overlap between those groups—which is very peculiar.

Is Jardina saying that there are lots of people who have very negative attitudes towards other races, but don't have a positive view of their own race? Yes, that's a possibility. There are a lot of cynical, nasty people who think that everybody is bad. They don't like blacks, but they don't particularly like white people either. That is a possible category of people. There are large numbers of people who might have negative attitudes towards other races but don't think that it would be at all permissible for whites to organize politically. They might be so politically inert that politics doesn't even enter their minds. They may just be annoyed with black people playing loud music, and that's all there is to it.

I want to understand the people who are ripe for white identity politics and yet don't really have any negative attitudes towards other racial groups. The question I basically have about these people is: Are they disingenuous, or are they clueless? Because if you believe that your group is a good thing and you strongly identify with it, and you believe that it's under threat, and you believe that it's okay to collectivize and organize to protect its interests, then exactly *against whom* are you protecting it?

If there's an "us," isn't there a "them"? And if you're really going to engage in identity politics, you've got to identify the "them," and eventually you might start drawing conclusions about "them" that could be negative. At the very least you have to draw the conclusion that they have different—i.e., conflicting—interests, or there's going to be no identity politics at all.

So something peculiar is going on here. I think white people just want to be nice. They want to think well of everybody. I think Prometheus in the legend was a white person. When Prometheus was chained to the Caucasus, and every day a vulture came to chew his liver out, he'd tell himself, "Well, you know, that vulture just has different interests than me, and he's got a nest full of little vultures at home he's trying to take care of, and I don't really blame him for what he's doing, and I don't want to make any anti-vulture generalizations." He'd feel bad about himself for drawing conclusions like that.

But as that vulture came back again and again, I think Prometheus would start taking a dim view of vulturekind. He might start out wanting to think the best of everyone, but when you're involved in an existential conflict, eventually you start feeling enmity towards other groups.

Right now white people are willing to engage in, or at least contemplate, identity politics, but they're not willing to contemplate what identity politics entails, which is actually fighting against other groups for dominance in a society. They haven't quite gotten there yet.

Now the big question that we face is: Is it possible to

have valid white identity politics that actually advances our ethnic interests, without ever getting people to fundamentally own up to the fact that politics involves us and them, conflict and harsh feelings?

Can we truly engage in identity politics and still be really nice? I think that's what a lot of our people want to do. That's my default preference. Can we get anywhere while leaving that preference intact, or are we going to have to radicalize people? Are we going to have to get them to be more serious about what it takes to preserve our interests in the face of ethnic displacement and ultimate ethnic annihilation?

The good news is that there are a lot of people who are now willing to consider white identity politics. The bad news is that they still want to be really nice. They want to think well of themselves. They want to think this isn't really that serious.

The great question that we face is: How much do we want to burst that bubble? How can we do that? And how can we do it without just coming off as grim, depressive madmen and inescapably marginal people—evil-minded, bloody-minded fanatics?

I think the time has come for our movement to start doing our own empirical research. I'm a philosopher. We do everything *a priori*. We stand way back. We don't do questionnaires. We don't do science. We stand back and interpret what scientists do. That's what I'm doing. I'm trying to put it in a larger political context.

But it's time for us to get serious about understanding the minds of the people that we want to save, because they are moving in our direction. And what's bringing them in our direction is not our brilliant, appealing websites and messages. In fact, most of these people are totally unaware of us. If 80% of white Americans are saying it's conceivably a good thing that whites should organize to protect their interests, believe me, that 80% has not been reading *Counter-Currents*. I see the numbers. We're read by a tiny fraction of that population.

So what's bringing them in our direction? It's not the magnetic force of our movement, which is largely unknown to them. It's the push of multiculturalism and globalization. The system is pushing people towards us.

This implies something very encouraging. The establishment wants to censor us. They think that the only reason multiculturalism isn't working is nay-sayers like me having a YouTube channel, or a Twitter account, or a website. But that's not true. Most of the people who are giving up on multiculturalism and globalization have never heard of us. They never saw a single tweet by Jared Taylor before Twitter shut him down.

What's driving these people towards us is the system's own policies, with their inevitable disastrous consequences and the lies and censorship required for the coverups. The system is not letting up on those policies. It continues to double down on them. Therefore, white ethnic consciousness will continue to rise, even if the system successfully censors every single explicit white advocate. That's a very encouraging thing.

Saving our people doesn't depend entirely on us. It depends on the fact that our people are basically wired the same way we are. There's a line from *The Dark Knight* where the Joker says, "We're not monsters; we're just ahead of the curve." We're not monsters for being ethnocentric. We're perfectly normal. We're just a little more sensitive than other people in our society. So ethnic displacement is bothering us first. But eventually it's going to bother everybody else, because they're fundamentally wired the same way that we are.[3]

That means that even if we can't reach them, they're

---

[3] Greg Johnson, "Ahead of the Curve," *In Defense of Prejudice*.

still going to draw the same conclusions when faced with the same data, and the facts are increasingly inescapable. It's increasingly hard to ignore the consequences of multiculturalism and globalization. So more and more of our people are going to be pushed in our direction.

But we need to understand what they're thinking. We need to understand how to bring them further along, how to deepen their awareness, and how to make it politically potent, so that we actually create the changes that we want.

That's my next project, and I think it should be a broader project of our movement. We now have trained academics who can do the same kind of analyses as Jardina and Eatwell and Goodwin. We need organizations. We need money. We really do need a think tank to try to lay the foundations for having a more scientific understanding of what's happening in the consciousness of our own people, and how we can then lead them forward to freedom and salvation—because that's ultimately what we want.

It's shocking and shameful that people who manufacture silly things—bracelets made out of candy, selfie sticks—have a more rigorous and fact-based understanding of the minds of the people that they're trying to reach and sell their product to than we, who represent the legitimate interests of our peoples and are trying to save them from extinction. It's because we haven't done the research yet. We haven't done the work. But there are interesting and encouraging clues coming out of academia that we can exploit. We should build our own research on their foundations.

Counter-Currents, August 19, 2019

The Identitarian Matrix*

Bring Back the Iron Curtain

I love visiting countries in Central and Eastern Europe. This is my first visit to Lithuania. I like it very much so far, and I want to implore all of you: Please bring back the Iron Curtain. Maybe get together in Warsaw, form a pact, and then bring back the Iron Curtain to protect this, the healthiest and best part of Europe, from the rot that is coming from the West.

I was asked to share my thoughts about how to create a Lithuanian nationalist youth movement. Now, I'm not young, and I'm not Lithuanian, but I like a challenge, so I accepted this task.

Of course, the way to begin to create something new in your country is to look around for examples of things that work in other countries. So you might look at Generation Identity in France or in Germany. You might look at CasaPound in Italy. You might look at Identity Evropa in the United States, or Students for Western Civilisation in Canada, and so forth.

But it is always dangerous to look to foreign models, because you don't want your nationalist movement to seem foreign. That would defeat the purpose. You want your nationalist movement to seem rooted in your nation.

So my recommendation is to smell all the flowers, gather some pollen, then retreat back to your hive and commune with the spirits of your ancestors, and try to

---

* This is a lightly edited transcription of my speech at the Kryptis Youth Conference in Vilnius, Lithuania, on February 15, 2019. I tried to remove wordiness and repetition and clarify some important points. I want to thank F. K. for transcribing it.

create something that's authentically Lithuanian. But there are a lot of examples to look to, and I want to direct you to some examples that I think are very useful.

THE ANTI-GLOBALIST CARNIVAL

There's a book called *The Struggle for the World* by Charles Lindholm and José Pedro Zúquete.[1] Lindholm is an American sociologist. Zúquete is a Portuguese political scientist. I read this book when it came out in 2010. It's about anti-globalization movements around the world, and I was most struck by the fact that there is a chapter on the European New Right. The European New Right is placed in the broader genus of anti-globalization movements, and when I read the chapter on the European New Right, I was struck by how meticulous and fair-minded the treatment was. I was most impressed by that.

I was very interested by this book's description of some Left-wing, anti-globalization movements. The first movement that really struck me was something called the World Social Forum. The World Social Forum began as a parody of the World Economic Forum, which meets in Davos, in Switzerland. The World Social Forum met for the first time in 2001, in a very run-down place in Brazil called Porto Alegre, which means "Happy Port." But Porto Alegre is a pretty down-at-its-heels, impoverished place, so the name is somewhat ironic.

A number of union organizers, Left-wing politicians, Left-wing academics, and anti-globalization activists got together and declared the World Social Forum. It was basically a parody of Davos. It turned out, though, that 15,000 people from all over the world showed up for this event. And when it was repeated in 2005, 155,000 people

---

[1] Charles Lindholm and José Pedro Zúquete, *The Struggle for the World: Liberation Movements for the 21st Century* (Stanford: Stanford University Press, 2010).

showed up. This was quite remarkable.

The World Social Forum was inspired by some examples of generally Left-wing but populist and grassroots anti-globalization movements that had taken place in the '90s.

For instance, in 1998, something called ATTAC arose in France. ATTAC was a grassroots movement demanding the regulation of financial markets for the good of consumers. In 1999, there was the great Battle of Seattle, in which 50,000 to 100,000 protesters shut down the city of Seattle and the World Trade Organization that was meeting there at the time. And in September 2000, the Global Day of Action took place in Prague at a meeting of the International Monetary Fund. The IMF was shut down by these protests, and the protests included a lot of street theater. For instance, one of the protests was a bunch of people dressed in pig masks playing soccer with the globe as a parody of what the International Monetary Fund is about.

Another group that inspired the World Social Forum is called CIRCA, which stands for Clandestine Insurgent Rebel Clown Army. CIRCA would do stunts, parody, and street theater to make fun of various globalist institutions and trends.

At the World Social Forum, something called the International Youth Camp, or IYC, emerged. The International Youth Camp was essentially a place where a bunch of young people who attended the forums camped out together. But it took on a life of its own and had a permanent carnival atmosphere.

What all these counter-globalization initiatives had in common was a non-hierarchical, distributed structure that made great use of the Internet to coordinate between independent actors, many of whom were anonymous and unknown to one another.

They also used street theater, as well as irony and

humor, to mock their enemies and to mobilize their supporters. There was a jazz-like performative structure to these movements. Individuals would take up certain common themes and play with them—mutate them, invert them, blend them with other themes—then throw them over to somebody else, who would do the same thing, then pass it on again.

Now, bear in mind that I was reading this in 2010, before the whole Alt Right phenomenon that we got to know in 2015 emerged. And when the Alt Right came along, I thought back to these Leftist anti-globalization activists, because the Alt Right had a similar structure and a similar ethos.

I was also wondering: Where have all these hilarious Leftists gone? Because by 2010, and much less by 2015, the people on the Left were a bunch of po-faced, sour, humorless, angry people. I don't think they could come up with anything like CIRCA anymore, and if they did, it would be a farce rather than a comedy. What had changed? Something had changed in the *Zeitgeist*.

These groups had created spaces, forums, camps, events as an incubator for anti-globalization ideas and activism. And these became very powerful. I saw a similar thing happening in our movement in 2015 and 2016, and I saw these groups as trailblazers. I doubt that they influenced the Alt Right, but it was an interesting example of parallel evolution.

Another model discussed by Zúquete and Lindholm is the international rave culture that started in the '90s. Raves are all-night or all-weekend drug-soaked techno-music festivals. But with rave organizers, there was a very conscious attempt to create an alternative to capitalist normality. Raves had a quasi-sacral quality to them. There was an attempt to create a different social and mental space removed from all the incentives of capitalism and globalism. And one of the things that was most interesting about the whole rave culture is that it was almost entirely white. Of course, techno music as a whole is a very white genre of music.

Despite its anti-globalist, anti-capitalist ethos, the rave scene was ultimately politically impotent. It led to nothing but a lot of partying. And once the rave is over, you have a hangover for a few days then go back to work, back to being cogs in the global economic system, and all your alienation doesn't change a thing. Raves were merely temporary alternatives to the global system. But they didn't have any revolutionary or socially transformative potential in the end.

There's a writer named Peter Lamborn Wilson, who also writes under the name of Hakim Bey. Hakim Bey wrote a book called *T.A.Z.: The Temporary Autonomous Zone.*[2] The Temporary Autonomous Zone is almost a theory of rave culture and what they were trying to create. They were trying to create a space that was autonomous from the incentives and pressures of bourgeois consumer-capitalist society. But we can create our own temporary autonomous zones as well, and if we do them well, they can have real revolutionary, transformative, social potential.

Identitarianism & the Spirit of Music

I want to draw your attention to another book. This is by José Pedro Zúquete on his own. It just came out, and it's called *The Identitarians: The Movement Against Globalism and Islam in Europe.*[3] This is a tremendously useful book. The author is so fair-minded, and asks so many

---

[2] Hakim Bey, *TAZ: The Temporary Autonomous Zone, Ontological Anarchy, Poetic Terrorism*, second ed. (Brooklyn: Autonomedia, 2003).

[3] José Pedro Zúquete, *The Identitarians: The Movement Against Globalism and Islam in Europe* (South Bend: Notre Dame University Press, 2018).

good questions, that I think he will be accused of being a sympathizer to Identitarianism, in a world where being a non-tendentious objective journalist almost makes you a fascist collaborator in the eyes of many. I've been following Identitarianism from the start, and even I learned a whole lot more about it from this book. All Identitarians need to read this book, especially if you're serious about creating an Identitarian movement in Lithuania or in any of the other Baltic states, or wherever you are from.

Two elements in the emergence of the Identitarian movement were quite striking to me.

One is the emphasis on the ethos of what could be called "boys' adventure tales." The ethos of adventure is contrary to the ethos of consumerism and bourgeois society. Your dad might want you to get a degree and get a job, whereas the spirit of adventure might drive you to take the money that he sends you for college, buy a ticket, and go join the French Foreign Legion. This is something Ernst Jünger did as a lad. The spirit of adventure is contrary to the spirit of our age, and the Identitarian movements consciously cultivate that adventurous spirit.

The other striking factor is the importance of music. Two of the most important Identitarian founders—and I am using "Identitarian" in a very broad sense, now—are Fabrice Robert in France and Gianluca Iannone in Italy. Robert created Generation Identity. Iannone created CasaPound.

Both of them started out running rock bands. Fabrice Robert ran a band called Fraction. Their music is described as a blend of ska, hardcore, and metal. I don't know what that would sound like. I need to go on YouTube and see if I can find some performances. Iannone still has his band. It is called ZetaZeroAlpha.

Back in the '90s, these two bands would tour together, which is very important, because today CasaPound and the Identitarian movement are aloof from one another.

They maintain a certain distance because CasaPound, being an Italian social movement, is openly fascist. For them, that is quite authentic to their tradition, because there was never a systematic suppression of fascist ideas and parties after the Second World War, and, in fact, fascist parties have always had men in parliament; people with fascist identifications and loyalties have held prominent positions in Italian society ever since the Second World War.

Therefore, for CasaPound, it is not hopelessly self-marginalizing to avow the fascist tradition, whereas Generation Identity very carefully tries to avoid any connection with any form of inter-war fascism. So they and CasaPound maintain a separation from one another. But if you look at the roots, these guys knew each other. They toured with one another. The birth of Identitarianism comes from the spirit of music. There is an important lesson here.

Why would musicians be particularly well-suited for politics? Musicians are performers. It's hard to get up and speak in front of people. There are many people who would rather die than get up in front of an audience and speak. And for those who do it, some of them are like me: Every fiber of my being screams against this. I don't enjoy this kind of stuff, honestly.

But there are some people who hunger for an audience, who hunger for attention. These are the kinds of people who become performers. They become actors. They become musicians. They want to get up on stage. They want your attention. Once they have the ability to read a room and connect with an audience and capture their attention, the next logical step for some of them is politics. There's a deep logic to that.

Another kind of person with the same set of skills is a priest. Priests have to be natural performers.

If you are doing pop music, youth music, you need to

have a connection with youth culture, and that's what we want, as well as a connection to a broader culture.

There are also certain skills that are presupposed by anyone who's a successful, even moderately successful, performer: a certain amount of entrepreneurial and managerial skills. Every band is a small business, and a lot of them fall apart because the people involved in them are only good at music, and they just can't keep track of the other stuff. If you have a long-term record of being a performer, oftentimes that means you have certain underlying practical skills that are keeping you in the game.

Those are very important skills. A lot of political groups fail because they have performers—leaders—but they don't have people who can balance a checkbook, file government reports, and things like that. Iannone and Robert probably had those entrepreneurial qualities and managerial skills, which are essential to political success.

Creating Alternative Spaces

There's another extremely important factor connecting priests and performers—musicians, actors—and that is the ability to create what I am going to call an "alternative mental space." Now, that may sound like a very vague notion, so let me try and make it a little clearer.

First of all: alternative to what?

In our case, we want an alternative to globalization, liberalism, homogenization, capitalism, and materialism. That whole complex of motives, that complex of ways of being, is inimical to nationalism and national populism. And yet, these are the powers that rule our world. So we're constantly trying to figure out how we can be nationalists and pay our bills, or not get doxed and fired, and so forth. The whole system is against us. And to project an alternative to that system, we have to find ways of getting our minds, and also our lives, outside of its clutches, if only for short periods of time. We have to figure out ways of creating national autonomous zones, Identitarian spaces.

Music festivals create such alternative spaces. Religious ceremonies do so as well.

The underlying distinction that generates religion is the sacred versus the profane. The profane world that we want to transcend is the world of globalization, liberalism, dumbing down, leveling out, and the destruction of our identities. An alternative to that could be understood as a sacred space, something above the profane world that we live in, where identity is an absolute value that cannot be priced—bought and sold—in terms of the filthy lucre of the global economic system.

Another way of understanding this alternative space is in terms of the carnival, which is always connected with religion, historically speaking. The carnival is a time when people can negate and invert established values and institutions. Thus, a lot of the street theater engaged in by these counter-globalization groups had a carnivalesque quality to it.

Perhaps the most important alternative to the bourgeois, global world, though, is what I prefer to call the "heroic world." And that's what we really need to aim at. We need to shift our minds from the priorities of people who think that the best life is a long and comfortable one, to the mindset of people who think that the best form of life is a heroic and responsible one, and who are willing to risk their comfort, their security, and even their physical existence for higher values. That is the ethos that will allow us to overturn this world.

Changing people's consciousness, changing the mind-space that people operate in, can sometimes be accomplished by changing the social space they're in. This is why rituals and festivals are politically very powerful things. When Richard Wagner wanted to transform

Germany from the roots up, he first looked back to a model from ancient Greece; he looked back to Greek tragedy.

Greek tragedy, it turns out, was an inherently religious activity. It was part of a greater religious festival. People would gather together as an audience, and on a stage—which was a sacred place—tragic dramas would be enacted. And these tragic dramas brought the deep identity of the participants to self-consciousness. Attic tragedy was about what it meant to be Greek. It was, therefore, a politically very potent thing, because bringing identity to consciousness can change the political world to better align with and express who we are. And that's our task.

So when Wagner decided that he wanted to transform Germany from the roots up, what did he do? He looked back into German myth and epic. Then he crafted music dramas. Then he created a festival, the Bayreuth Festival, which was modeled on the Dionysia of Athens, where Greek tragedy was born. The Festival was designed to attract Germany's elites into a space and an experience that would allow them to come to a deeper understanding of their identity, and on the basis of that, he hoped for a transformation of German culture and politics.

This is deep metapolitics. And interestingly enough, the term "metapolitics" was coined in the pages of the journal published at Bayreuth, under the editorship of Wagner's son-in-law, Houston Stewart Chamberlain.

So what does this all mean for you? Well, if you know any musical geniuses, get in touch with them.

The key to creating an Identitarian movement is to create social spaces and activities outside the contemporary global system that allow the participants to come to consciousness of their identity, that uphold identity as something sacred, as the highest political value, and that can mobilize this new consciousness for political change.

The Limits of Play

One thing I want to caution you against, though, is too much frivolity, specifically making irony into an ethos.[4] The Alt Right and also the World Social Forum and aligned movements very heavily employ comedy, mockery, parody, irony, and so forth. These are very powerful tools of deconstructing your enemy. When you mock your enemy, you demoralize them, and you also feel empowered. Whenever you can laugh at something, that's a sign that on some level, you feel superior to it.

And this is why it was an important sign when all the humor went out of the Left. It means that they're already psychologically defeated. They're in a kind of snarling, retreating stance. They're like protesters who are scrunched up on the ground as the police rain down blows with their truncheons. They're not in a position of mastery and self-confidence anymore. Psychologically, they're under siege, and we're on the attack, because we're funny, and they're not.

They're not funny; they're merely laughable. People are laughing at them. People are laughing with us. And whenever they try to turn the tables on us, it's incredibly lame, because they've lost their sense of being above us. And that's a huge advantage we need to press.

But in the end, irony is only a tool. It is a way of moving in the right direction. It is useful for mocking your enemies. It is also useful for creating a safe mental space where people can try on radical new ideas. It is the equivalent of going to a store and trying on a shirt to see if it looks good on you. You're not committed to it. If it doesn't look good, you put it back on the rack. Or taking a car for a test drive, or buying something with a thirty-day, money-back guarantee.

---

[4] Greg Johnson, "Identity vs. Irony," *From Plato to Postmodernism.*

If you can give people spaces or options where they do not have to commit 100% to something, they are more likely to try it, and if they're more likely to try it, they're more likely to buy it. And irony and ironic spaces are extremely important for that.

But ultimately, the ethos that we want is not the carnivalesque ethos, it's the heroic ethos. And heroism does not draw anything from being non-committal—one foot in, one foot out—which is what irony is. Heroism requires 110% commitment, and irony as an ethos undermines that. It's a very useful tool, but we have to keep it in check.

Another important thing to bear in mind is one of the big mistakes of the Alt Right in America: trying to take the memes and irony off the Internet and to do it in the real world. First of all, it doesn't look good in the real world, and second, it collapsed a very useful distinction between dignified and plausible public representatives of our ideas, and a bunch of scruffy, anonymous, unwashed, vicious, but hilarious people on the Web.

As long as there is a space between these groups, the respectable, responsible public advocates could say, "I regret the excesses of our more enthusiastic brethren, but, you know, they do have a point." That allows you to maintain your dignity, your public standing, and your political viability. But when those two worlds came together and the distinction collapsed, we had a problem.

All was well when Alt Right Twitter-trolls were triggering journalists, and journalists were writing furious, coked-up *Buzzfeed* diatribes saying, "All these people are a bunch of horrible *Nazis*," and then people would Google the person and find . . . Jared Taylor. And they would not see a horrible Nazi, but a reasonable guy who sounds disturbingly sensible. Whenever that happened—and it happened a lot—it undermined the establishment narrative.

But when you can Google the story, and, ohmigod!, there's actual footage of somebody behaving exactly like the *Buzzfeed* reporters say, that doesn't undermine the media's credibility, it reinforces it. It also undermines our ability to play the game in which we can benefit from the energy of the trolls but maintain the dignity and seriousness that's ultimately necessary if we're going to gin up that heroic ethos to win.

So again: create alternative spaces, be authentic, don't make your nationalist movement seem foreign, and take inspiration wherever you can get it. But if it seems foreign, keep it esoteric. And the main reason to do that is because ultimately, we believe that ethnonationalism is rooted in nature, in objective reality. It's also rooted in the healthy part of any national tradition. And if you can find a way of rooting ethnonationalism in nature, which is common to us all, and to things that are authentically part of your own national tradition, you will be able to connect better with your people. And that's ultimately the most important thing: to connect with your people, if you're going lead your people to safety.

In their Hearts, they Know We're Right

One last thing that you need to keep in mind: I remember when I first learned to ride a bicycle, my dad put training wheels on it. I was just a little kid, but I remember realizing that it was going to take an act of will, an act of self-confidence on my part, to kick aside the training wheels.

I want to argue that everything you, as Lithuanians, will learn from books like Zúquete's *The Identitarians*, or from me, or from Jared Taylor, or online, or wherever you encounter ideas, everything you're going to learn from outside to help create your Identitarian movement is going to be like training wheels. But eventually, you've got to kick those training wheels away.

And what's going to sustain you when you take that leap, that act of will? The thing that sustains me, and that sustains all of us, is the following conviction.

Years ago, when Barry Goldwater was running for President of the United States, Charlton Heston, a famous actor who became a conservative, was making a movie somewhere in Southern California. Whenever he was picked up in the morning in a limo and whisked off to work, he would see a Barry Goldwater billboard that said, "In your heart, you know he's right." He would see this billboard every day, coming and going, and at a certain point, it hit him. He said, "Sonofabitch! He *is* right!"

And I've always thought it would be a really great, kind of douchey, move on my part to title one of my books *In Your Heart, You Know I'm Right*. But that is something I truly believe, something that we have to believe. What we stand for is not only based on nature, but we must have faith that our people are not so poorly constituted by nature that they don't have the ability to see and value what's natural. It would be very weird if an organism came into the world, and needed to go with the grain of nature to survive, but didn't have the ability to recognize what goes with the grain of nature.

We have to believe that all of our people basically believe what we believe. We're not monsters; we're just ahead of the curve.[5] That's a very important thing to keep in mind: We're just a little more ethnocentric and a little more sensitive than your mother or your father or your neighbor, or whoever is the first normie that pops into your head. They're not another species. They are our own flesh and blood, and they are constituted in the same way: to feel comfortable around people who are like them and a little anxious around people who are different.

---

[5] Greg Johnson, "Ahead of the Curve," *In Defense of Prejudice*.

We know that's how the brain works. They might have a lot of ideas in their forebrain programmed into them by their college and their minister and Hollywood, that conflict with those intuitions, but we all believe those things. In their hearts, they know we're right.

So when you get your formula together to create an Identitarian youth movement, and you try on various things for size, and you come up with a workable model, and you say, "Okay, we're going to try this!"—at a certain point, you will kick away the training wheels, and you have to be sustained by the assumption that all those people out there, that you are trying to help, in their hearts, they know you're right.

Counter-Currents, April 10, 2019

The Uppity White Folks Manifesto

White people are ready for white identity politics. This is clear from the rise of populist and nationalist politicians and parties around the white world, as well as the research of political scientist Ashley Jardina, which shows that significant numbers of white Americans have positive racial identities, believe the current system is anti-white, reject white guilt, and think it is appropriate for whites to politically organize to protect their collective interests.[1]

This is encouraging news, because it means that the metapolitical conditions for white identity politics are crystallizing. Center-Right parties, however, refuse to cross the line into explicit white identity politics because they are part of a globalist elite that regards white nationalism and populism as the top threats to their hegemony. But that is also encouraging news, for it is an opportunity for genuine white identitarians to establish themselves as a political force.

In *The White Nationalist Manifesto*, I outlined how we might restore or create homogeneously white homelands.[2] But the vast majority of people who are ready for white identity politics are not ready for full-on White Nationalism.

I use the phrase "uppity white folks" for the people who are ready for white identity politics but not (yet) ready for White Nationalism. They need a manifesto as well. I'm not the guy to write it. I will stick to White Nationalism. But I

---

[1] Ashley Jardina, *White Identity Politics* (New York: Cambridge University Press, 2019), esp. chapter 3.

[2] Greg Johnson, "Restoring White Homelands," *The White Nationalist Manifesto*.

do have three suggestions for turning uppity white folks into a political force.

1. Make Multiculturalism Work for You

If you don't aim at a white ethnostate, then you are committed to some form of multiculturalism. So you need to make it work for you. Under the present system, however, multiculturalism works only for non-whites, who are encouraged to cultivate group identities and assert them in the political realm. Whites, however, are barred from this. That would be "racism," and racism is the worst thing in the world—but only when practiced by white people, specifically the white majority or founding stock of any given white nation.

Under the present dispensation, it is okay even for white minorities to practice identity politics in white nations. So Swedes can practice identity politics in Finland, but not in Sweden. And Finns can practice identity politics in Sweden, but not in Finland. Being Finnish is an approved ethnic identity in Sweden. Being Swedish is an approved ethnic identity in Finland. But Finns in Finland must define their identity in terms of universal values like openness and tolerance, and Swedes in Sweden must do exactly the same thing. Thus white ethnic identity is good only when it is useful in undermining ethnically defined white states, never good when it is used to maintain them.

This is a morally outrageous double standard, since it puts whites at a systematic disadvantage in their own homelands. If it is legitimate for minorities of all races to be politically selfish, while white majorities are allowed only to think about the common good, that is a recipe for exploitation. Identity politics for white majorities is *moral*, because it is fair. It is *necessary*, in order to prevent exploitation. And, since whites will eventually tire of unfairness and exploitation, white identity politics is *inevitable* as well.

But you can't stop with mere equality. You need to

demand *special privileges*. Bear with me. This isn't as bad as it sounds. Not all peoples can be equal in a multicultural society. For instance, in Spain, the dominant language is Spanish. In Sweden, it is Swedish. Is this "fair" if you are a Finn living in Sweden or an Englishman living in Spain? Yes and no.

Obviously, no society can treat all the languages of the world as equal. Life would simply grind to a halt. Thus one has to privilege the dominant language.

Or languages, because in Spain the Basques and Catalonians have their own languages, and they naturally resent Spanish imperialism. The Basques and Catalonians demand special privileges as indigenous minorities, and the Spaniards have wisely granted them. If they didn't, it would strengthen Basque and Catalonian separatism.

Most people have no moral objections to *special privileges for indigenous minorities*. The same is true for what can be called *historically established minorities*, for instance Germans in Hungary or Swedes in Finland. Such populations exist in practically every white society due to historical contingencies like conquests, migrations, and sloppy partitions. Such privileges are a central feature of all multicultural orders.

But for some reason, whites are no longer comfortable with demanding *special privileges for the people who founded the state*: Spaniards in Spain, Swedes in Sweden, the French in France, (white) Americans in America, (Anglo) Canadians in Canada, (Anglo) New Zealanders in New Zealand, and so forth.

Such privileges objectively exist, of course, for all those born to the dominant linguistic and cultural stocks of these societies. It is a privilege to grow up in a country where one is part of the founding group, so that nothing about the language, culture, history, and public spaces is alien to you.

But people have been taught that asserting and defending these privileges is the moral outrage of "supremacism."

It was wrong for the Japanese to impose themselves on the Chinese and Koreans. It was wrong for the French to impose themselves on Indochina and Africa. It was wrong for the Spaniards to impose themselves on the Aztecs and Incas.

But how did we get to the point where Japanese supremacism is "problematic" in Japan, French supremacism in France, Spanish supremacism in Spain, etc.? Why *shouldn't* peoples be supreme in their own homelands, as long as other peoples are not denied the same privileges in their homelands?

As for indigenous minorities, fairness requires they either be granted their own homelands or maximum autonomy in their local affairs.

But both founding populations and indigenous minorities should reject the absurd idea of granting civic equality to the entire population of the globe. The only thing we owe foreigners is respect for their basic human rights.

Multiculturalism means different group identities and different group privileges within the same society. To make multiculturalism work for the founding population, they need to assert their special privileges as the founding stock and resist the demographic and cultural erosion of their status.

In practical terms, what would that mean? Let's take the United States for example, although of course the same principles apply to all counties. An American identitarian movement should make three basic demands.

First, *the American state must halt and reverse the demographic decline of Americans in America.* And by "Americans" we all understand *white* Americans, the founding stock of the country. In 1965, when America opened its doors to non-white immigration, it was 90% white. Today, the white population is barely over 60%. Because of non-white immigration, low white American fertility, and high non-white fertility, with each passing year, those numbers get worse for white Americans.

American identitarians should demand that, each year, the white American percentage of the American population be a bit larger than the year before. This would entail social and political programs directed specifically to the demographic benefit of white Americans and not other groups.

For instance, the American state would reduce the immigration of non-whites and increase their emigration (for instance by repatriating refugees and reunifying immigrant families in their homelands). It would also reduce incentives for white Americans to emigrate. If white American birthrates are below those of non-white populations, the state should create programs to specifically increase white American birthrates.

Once such policies are in place, the creeping decline of America will be replaced with a creeping renewal. It took half a century to make America into a multicultural dystopia. It might take half a century to fix it. In the meantime, Americans can go about their business as usual, but with the optimism that comes from knowing that their progeny have a bright future ahead, not decline and extinction.

As for the objection that it is unfair to discriminate against non-whites, first, it is completely fair to promote the well-being of a people in its own homeland; it does not prevent other peoples from doing the same in their homelands; second, under the present system, the American government treats non-whites better than white Americans. Why should they have special privileges? If any group should have special privileges in America, shouldn't it be white Americans, the people who founded the country? That's what it is to have a homeland.

Second, *the American state must promote the well-being of white Americans in America*. The American state should be committed to making sure that every year, white Americans enjoy a better quality of life. This requires social and political programs tailored to the well-being of white Americans and not other groups. A country that cared about its founding stock would not, for instance, let social problems like the mass "deaths of despair" and the opioid epidemic affecting white Americans to go unnoticed and unaddressed.

Third, *the American state must secure the cultural dominance and enrichment of white Americans in America.* This means that the American state should make the American language, history, and culture *normative* in America *for whites and non-whites alike.*

Why shouldn't Americans have a homeland called America? Why shouldn't the American language and culture be normative in America? Why shouldn't the American state prioritize the genetic and cultural interests of Americans? Why shouldn't American identity and history be reflected in the public realm in America? Why shouldn't visiting America, or residing there as a foreigner, be contingent on respecting the American people and their language, culture, and values? That's what it means to have a homeland.

Yet this sort of nationalism is rejected by the entire cultural and political establishment in America and most other white countries. That is the madness of the multiculturalism that has entranced white nations into marching, lemming-like, to their biological and cultural extinction.

2. Ninety-Percent White Nationalism

If an American identitarian movement were to propose reversing the demographic decline of white America, they would need a target number. If the public is not yet ready for homogeneously white ethnostates, that target number must be somewhere under 100%. As an American, I would choose 90%. In 1965, before America abandoned immigration policies that were committed to maintaining a white supermajority, the US was about 90% white.

As for the ethnic breakdown of the non-white percentage, I would leave that completely open. I would, however, make it clear that it could contain representatives of all currently existing non-white groups. This is important to reduce opposition.

First, many whites who are ready for some form for white identity politics will not accept it unless you leave some room for "based" minority outliers, mail-order brides, indigenous minorities, hard-luck groups like refugees and the descendants of slaves, and the purveyors of their favorite ethnic cuisines.

Second, leaving some space for all existing outsider groups would reduce resistance among such populations. Many outsiders might not resist the end of multiculturalism. They might even welcome it. After all, they want to live in white countries because of their white characteristics—high standards of living, law and order, etc.—and they see that these are threatened by multiculturalism. Multiculturalism is just the white majority being gaslighted into a long, drawn-out suicide, with another Third World hellhole at the end of the road. Intelligent non-whites who have escaped such societies don't want to inflict them on their posterity. But they would resist white identity politics if no provision were made for their kind in the future.

This kind of policy seems fair to all parties. Majorities get their homelands back: Denmark for Danes, Hungary for Hungarians, America for Americans, etc. Indigenous and historically established minority groups have a place as well. Even members of more recent immigrant populations can envision a place for themselves. And if they do not want to live as outsiders in a normatively white America, they have homelands to which they can return, and we should give them generous incentives to do so. Everybody has a place, everybody has a future, everybody's interests are taken into account.

Ninety-percent White Nationalism can even deliver a reasonable facsimile of 100% White Nationalism. The ethnostate is the idea of a racially and culturally homogeneous homeland for a particular people. But how homogeneous is homogeneity? In my chapter on "Homogeneity" in *The White Nationalist Manifesto,* I distinguish three senses of the term:

- *Strict homogeneity*—meaning there are no racial and cultural outsiders at all
- De facto *homogeneity*—meaning that outsiders are present, but citizens are not forced to deal with them, so if one wants, one can live *as if* one inhabits a strictly homogeneous society
- *Normative homogeneity*—meaning that if outsiders are present, they accept and live by the norms of the dominant group.

Most white societies will reject strict homogeneity. European colonial societies usually have aboriginal relict populations. Others have descendants of slaves and indentured servants. Still others have long-established minority groups like Swedes in Finland. Strict homogeneity just seems unfair to these groups. Beyond that, most white societies are fine with small numbers of foreign residents, foreign students, foreign tourists, and assimilable immigrants.

However, the presence of such people is no threat to a society if it is committed to normative and *de facto* forms of homogeneity. A 90% American America can still be 100% normatively American. A 90% American America can also allow Americans complete freedom of association and disassociation, so that nobody is forced to deal with outsiders if he prefers to remain separate. Thus people in a 90% White Nationalist society can, if they so choose, live *as if* it is a 100% White Nationalist society, which should satisfy most people.

Some of the most vocal opponents of 90% White Nationalism will be advocates of the 100% variety. The poison pill for them is the Jewish question, for Jews are long-established minorities in practically every white society. Jews are the leading proponents of multiculturalism and race-replacement immigration. If these policies are rejected, most Jews will feel uncomfortable. Many might even emigrate. But some might remain among the 10%. That possibility might reduce Jewish opposition to 90% White Nationalism, but it will guarantee the opposition of hardcore anti-Semites. Such opposition might, however, improve the overall political prospects of 90% White Nationalism.

3. Medicare for All Plus Slurs

After setting out clear goals, the next step is to gain the power needed to enact your policies. To do that, you must put together a winning political coalition. But that might prove surprisingly easy. It may be as simple as giving the people what they already want.

A very large chunk of the electorate in most white countries is "populist." Populists have two main traits. First, they are somewhat socially conservative and patriotic. Second, they want an interventionist state to protect the interests of the working and middle classes from the elites. Thus they favor social safety nets and barriers to economic globalization.

Our ruling elites want the exact opposite: social liberalism and globalism, including economic globalization, which enriches the elites by allowing them access to cheap labor through both immigration and offshoring.

The current political system is perfectly calibrated to

maintain the illusion of democracy while consistently *not* giving the people what they want: social conservatism and the interventionist state. Instead, the political system reliably gives the elites more of what they want: social liberalism and globalization.

This elite consensus is often called "neoliberalism." Jonathan Bowden described it as a Left-wing oligarchy, a hyper-stratified form of capitalism married to Left-wing identity politics, which is no longer about promoting socialism for the working class. Instead, it is about promoting upward mobility *within capitalism* for previously marginalized groups.

The people are never given the choice of voting for a platform that gives them exactly what they want: social conservatism and the interventionist state. Instead, the center-Left offers an interventionist state combined with social liberalism. The center-Right offers conservatism combined with pro-business policies.

Given this setup, you'd think that as the Left and Right trade power, the people would get at least half of what they want all the time. But somehow it doesn't work out that way. When the Left is in power, it is more effective at delivering the half of its platform favored by the elites: social liberalism. When the Right is in power, it is also more effective at delivering the half of its platform favored by the elites: tax cuts for the rich, free trade, open borders, etc.

A system in which the majority get *none of what they want, all the time* cannot be seriously described as a democracy.

But as long as the people have the right to vote, we can change this system. Let's look at some numbers. The populist voting bloc varies from country to country. It also varies depending on how one measures it. A 2015 study of the American electorate by Lee Drutman is highly suggestive.[3] Drutman mapped voters on two axes: their attitudes toward *Social Security* (a welfare-state measure highly popular among working- and middle-class voters) and *immigration* (a key trait of globalization).

The populist electorate favored maintaining or increasing Social Security while maintaining or decreasing immigration. This turned out to be 40.3% of the electorate, the single largest bloc. Liberals and Leftists, who favor maintaining or increasing both Social Security and immigration, are 32.9%. Moderates, defined as those who wish to maintain Social Security and immigration at present levels, are 20.5%. "Neoliberals" and free-market conservatives are defined as those who support increasing immigration and lowering Social Security. They constitute just 6.2% of the electorate. Yet their preferences have been consistently triumphing since the late 1980s.

Identitarian populists already have the largest voting bloc on our side: 40.3%. All we need is to win over 10% more of the electorate from liberals and moderates. This should be possible because they want contradictory things: both immigration and Social Security, or, more broadly: both globalization and an interventionist state that promotes the interests of the masses.

But you can't have both. You can't have open borders and free trade as well as high wages and the welfare state. Open borders lower wages and overburden the welfare state. Free trade means dismantling barriers to a single global price for labor, which means pauperizing workers in the First World.

The economic consequences of globalization are clear to anyone who knows basic microeconomics.[4] It should be

---

[3] Lee Drutman, "What Donald Trump Gets About the Electorate," *Vox*, August 18, 2015.

[4] For more on this, see my essay "The End of Globalization," *Truth, Justice, & a Nice White Country*.

possible to convince moderates and even some liberals and Leftists that they want incompatible things. Then we must force them to choose. If forced to choose, most will choose First World prosperity and the welfare state over globalization. But we don't even need to convince the majority of them. Based on Drutman's numbers, we need to convince only one in five liberals and moderates to create a solid electoral majority. We can do that.

I have two caveats about Drutman's analysis.

First, elections are naturally fought on more than just two issues. But if you were to poll the electorate on their attitudes toward the welfare state and free trade, or government healthcare and political correctness, or environmental regulations and interventionist foreign policy, you would find roughly the same breakdowns. Populists want a stronger welfare state plus less free trade. They want more government healthcare and less political correctness. They want a cleaner environment and an America-first foreign policy. In sum, populists want nationalism, patriotism, and social conservatism plus an interventionist state that looks out for the majority.

Second, Drutman's issues—Social Security and immigration—can be analyzed purely in economic populist terms. But, as Roger Eatwell and Matthew Goodwin argue in *National Populism*, economics is not the sole force driving the rise of national populism. Today's populists don't oppose immigration simply because it lowers wages. They also oppose it for identitarian reasons. Immigration is changing their homelands beyond recognition. It is endangering the future of their nations. Thus they want it stopped. Identity, moreover, is not just a contributing factor in modern populism. For many, it is the decisive factor. Indeed, many people would prefer to preserve their national identity and sovereignty even if it makes them less prosperous. By emphasizing identity as well as economics, an identitarian populist movement can appeal to more people and also motivate them to sacrifice economically for its cause.

What would an American identitarian populist movement offer the Right? Patriotism. Social conservatism. An end to political correctness. An America-first foreign policy, which means fewer wars. It would not offer the Right more libertarian economics (including open borders) and neoconservative global interventionism. But those views are unpopular even on the Right.

What would an American populist movement offer the center and the Left? State intervention in the economy, including a welfare state, to help the working and middle classes. Environmentalism. Massive spending on education, infrastructure, and research and development, including space exploration. An America-first foreign policy, which means fewer wars. It would not offer the Left open borders, political correctness, and anti-white identity politics. But those are not all that popular even on the Left.

In short, identitarian populism would offer "Medicare for all + slurs," a phrase that was coined as a parody but sounds like a platform to me.[5]

The free-market Right has long used immigration as a cynical weapon against the welfare state. You can't have open borders and a functioning welfare state. An identitarian populist movement should use the welfare state as a cynical weapon against immigration and neoliberalism more broadly.

Conventional free-market Rightists reject a Scandinavian-style welfare state in America because they fear it would become a fiscal black hole. From a populist point of view, that would be a virtue. A new raft of highly popular entitlements could be used to suck dry centers of elite power: the military-industrial complex, big business, and academia.

---

[5] To quote a Tweet by Sean P. McCarthy.

One could fund a welfare state through tariffs on foreign manufactured goods and confiscatory taxation of the super-rich, especially those who made their fortunes through outsourcing and open borders. An insatiable welfare state could be used to defund foreign aid, interventions, and wars. It could also gobble up subsidies to higher education. Finally, to keep such a welfare state sustainable, a nation would have to close its borders and repatriate tens of millions of illegal immigrants. That's a plan worth trusting.

This is just a sketch of how an identitarian populist movement could mobilize tens of millions of uppity white Americans who think some form of white identity politics is necessary and moral, even though they are not ready to consider more radical White Nationalist positions like the ethnostate. But these people are still rejected by the political establishment, which holds that identity politics for whites—and only whites—is simply immoral.

Tens of millions of white Americans are realizing that they have no political representation. They increasingly understand that the political system is not just designed to ignore them but to replace them. They are angry and searching for alternatives. This presents an enormous opportunity to talented and ambitious political outsiders. Whoever mobilizes these millions will write the next chapter in the history of American populism.

Counter-Currents, November 5 & 18, &
December 17, 2020

INDEX

About the Author

Greg Johnson, Ph.D. is Editor-in-Chief of Counter-Currents Publishing Ltd., as well as the *Counter-Currents* webzine (http://www.counter-currents.com/).

He is the author of *Confessions of a Reluctant Hater* (San Francisco: Counter-Currents, 2010; second, expanded ed., 2016); *New Right vs. Old Right* (Counter-Currents, 2013); *Truth, Justice, & a Nice White Country* (Counter-Currents, 2015); *In Defense of Prejudice* (Counter-Currents, 2017); *You Asked for It: Selected Interviews*, vol. 1 (Counter-Currents, 2017); *The White Nationalist Manifesto* (Counter-Currents, 2018; second ed., 2019); *Toward a New Nationalism* (Counter-Currents, 2019); *From Plato to Postmodernism* (Counter-Currents, 2019); *It's Okay to Be White* (Hollywood: Ministry of Truth, 2020); *Graduate School with Heidegger* (Counter-Currents, 2020); and *Here's The Thing: Selected Interviews*, vol. 2 (Counter-Currents, 2020).

Under the pen name Trevor Lynch, he is the author of *Trevor Lynch's White Nationalist Guide to the Movies* (Counter-Currents, 2012), *Son of Trevor Lynch's White Nationalist Guide to the Movies* (Counter-Currents, 2015), *Return of the Son of Trevor Lynch's CENSORED Guide to the Movies* (Counter-Currents, 2019), and *Trevor Lynch: Part Four of the Trilogy* (Counter-Currents, 2020).

He has also edited many books, including *North American New Right*, vol. 1 (Counter-Currents, 2012); *North American New Right*, vol. 2 (Counter-Currents, 2017); *Dark Right: Batman Viewed from the Right* (with Gregory Hood) (Counter-Currents, 2018); and *The Alternative Right* (Counter-Currents, 2018).

His writings have been translated into Czech, Danish, Dutch, Estonian, Finnish, French, German, Greek, Hungarian, Norwegian, Polish, Portuguese, Russian, Slovak, Spanish, Swedish, and Ukrainian.

www.ingramcontent.com/pod-product-compliance
Lightning Source LLC
LaVergne TN
LVHW020110221224
799600LV00001B/66